WINE MAKING

A Guide to Growing, Nurturing and Producing

WINE MAKING

A Guide to Growing, Nurturing and Producing

Kieron Atkinson and Jane Travis

FOREWORD BY OZ CLARKE

THE CROWOOD PRESS

First published in 2021 by
The Crowood Press Ltd
Ramsbury, Marlborough
Wiltshire SN8 2HR

enquiries@crowood.com

www.crowood.com

British Library Cataloguing-in-Publication Data
A catalogue record for this book is available from the British Library.

ISBN 978 1 78500 969 3

Illustrations by Sara Naylor.

Typeset by Simon and Sons

Cover design by Blue Sunflower Creative

Printed and bound in India by Parksons Graphics

CONTENTS

FOREWORD BY OZ CLARKE

In my lifetime, I am certain that there has never been a time like this, when we, as a nation and as individuals, need to be as self-sufficient as we can. Brexit became a reality in 2021. Regardless of our political views, this is a time when we must all set out to make the best of our country and one way we can do this is to support those who produce our national foods and drinks.

There are many products that Britain creates to as high a standard as any in the world. Our fish, our shellfish, our grass-fed lamb and beef, our crisp, delicious fruits; our pies and our cheeses – we now have more different cheeses than France! When it comes to drink, no country in the world makes more types of drink to such a high standard. Beers, ciders, perries, gins, brandies and whiskies.

Oz Clarke OBE, author of *English Wine: From Still to Sparkling*.

And wine. There has been a sea change in the quality of our wine, currently in England and Wales, but the Scots and the Northern Irish are not to be counted out in the near future. Not only is the quality of our sparkling wine unquestionably world class – even the French are having to admit that – but our still wines can now be breathtakingly good, pure and bright, as cool as winter sunshine, as fresh as springtime dew on an early daffodil. Climate change is a global threat, but in this small corner of the Earth it is creating possibilities to plant grapes and make wine in almost every English county and in many of those in Wales, too.

Kieron Atkinson is someone I have greatly enjoyed working with on English wine projects. Not only is he a supreme craftsman and expert, but he has a very special quality – a vision of flavour for each vineyard and each winery with whom he works. He takes the time and makes the effort to understand the vineyard and its possibilities, but also the hopes and aspirations of the owners.

English and Welsh wine has the chance to be unique in its character and flavour. Kieron understands this and achieves remarkable results across the length and breadth of the nation, from the banks of the River Tyne to Cornwall.

With this book, Kieron takes you on a journey, from choosing a site, to deciding which vine varieties are suitable, to considering what types of winery equipment are necessary or desirable and how to use them. And, above all, he helps you to visualize what flavours, what perfumes, what thrilling local, individual characteristics you might want your wine to possess.

Kieron works with projects both little and large. This book will be invaluable, even if you are only making a tiny splash of wine in a couple of demijohns. Every winemaker in our nation can be part of the Great British Wine Revolution, however great or small their enterprise.

This book shows you how to care for your vines and perfect your winemaking skills, but above all it will give you the confidence to grab the reins and 'go for it'. With Kieron as your guide, you will be in for a fantastic ride.

Oz Clarke, 12 January 2021

PREFACE

ABOUT KIERON ATKINSON

In summer 2007, I was an Army officer serving in Afghanistan in the Upper Gereshk Valley. This was about as unforgiving a place as you can imagine and as extreme as it is beautiful. Whilst there and throughout that operational tour, I made a promise to myself that if I were to return home, I would go on to do whatever work I wanted, without too much consideration of the financial return, but focused on a way of life I wanted to follow.

As my considerations widened, I also decided that I wanted to make something and have an outdoor element to my work. I parked this thought for a further two years whilst becoming a tactics instructor at the Land Warfare School in Warminster and it was only by chance that my thoughts turned to wine production whilst visiting the south-west of France and a small producer, Jonathan Hesford at Domaine Treloar. Jon showed me and my wife around his winery and vineyard and offered that I should visit over the harvest period for an extended time. I returned two months later; I actually missed most of the harvest, but did get to see how the business operated and what this lifestyle entailed.

The following winter I volunteered at Renishaw Hall Vineyard, a modest in size yet historic vineyard

Kieron Atkinson, wine maker and vineyard consultant.

situated under 10 miles from Sheffield city centre, then enrolled at Plumpton College on a two-year wine-production course. Whilst at Plumpton, I also worked for the Rothschilds and Waddesdon Wine under the excellent MD Christopher Campbell, who showed me what the world of wine sales involved and I carried out numerous tastings of the fantastic and celebrated Rothschild wines. By this stage, it was clear that I was bitten by the wine bug. However, it was in production and growing the vines where my passion lay – I was interested in how it got into the bottle, not just drinking it!

Whilst at college, a number of further opportunities presented themselves. First, I took on Renishaw Hall Vineyard as my own project – Renishaw Hall wine is now selling all over the country, winning national and international awards and being sold into major retailers. It is also a thriving tourism business that draws thousands of visitors each year. Second, I became a contract wine maker at Halfpenny Green Wine Estate in the West Midlands, owned by Clive Vickers. This experience meant that I was part of a team now producing well over 100,000 bottles per year and working with over twenty different vineyards in the process. It also meant that I got to produce just about every type of wine out there – from still and sparkling, through to *Pét-Nat*.

I combined these skills and experiences to start the English Wine Project. This is a consultancy business that covers all aspects of production from vineyard establishment, winemaking, wine sales, tourism and wider wine consultancy. We are expanding all the time and, at the time of writing, have a production facility producing English wines and ciders in Darley Abbey in Derbyshire.

I hope that this book helps you – and will allow you to get to grips with the basics of wine production. It is a truly exciting time to be involved in the industry as it grows and becomes the weighty international player that the weather, professional knowledge and consumer appeal predicts it will.

ABOUT JANE TRAVIS

Jane Travis has worked in writing and communications for over twenty years. She combines her love of working with words with working in the vineyard whenever time allows. Her career background is in heritage estates, travel and tourism, where she joins Kieron as an advocate for all the amazing food and drink experiences that the UK provides.

When Jane is not out in the vineyard or at her desk writing, she loves countryside walks and exploring new places with her family, relishing the Great Outdoors whenever possible.

Jane Travis wrapping up as warm as possible in the vineyard.

Vines growing at Carlton Towers in Yorkshire.

INTRODUCTION

'Grow your own' is seeing a renaissance, with households across the UK producing fruit and vegetables from their own garden plots, allotments or even a sunny windowsill. Grapes are no exception. Whether a single vine in a garden greenhouse or a full-blown vineyard of several acres, grape growing is on the rise. And from grapes, of course, comes the ancient and globally adored drink: wine.

Kieron and son Hugh bringing the harvest in at Renishaw Hall Vineyard.

There's never been a stronger time for UK wine producers – long gone are the days of English wine being snorted at as nothing better than for use in cooking. There are currently over 700 vineyards[1] across England and Wales and the industry is worth upward of £130 million, with more vineyard sites being planted each year. These slick, professional set-ups are producing globally award-winning wines that are regularly knocking the likes of Champagne off the top spot.

Additionally, the sometimes dubious label given to home-produced wine has also gradually faded, with the growth in popularity of artisan food and drink producers. Visit a food fair today, and locally made drinks sell as well as the jams, cheeses and pies. Go to a supermarket, and the number of 'craft' drinks vying for shelf space with bigger brands is clear. Consumers are recognizing that it is not only on trend to eat and drink produce made locally and in smaller batches, but kinder to the planet, too.

Whether it's a dozen bottles of wine created with love from your kitchen table, or thousands of cases produced from a commercial vineyard; the care and attention are the same. This book will guide you through the processes, the challenges, the fun and the satisfaction to expect – as you 'grow your own wine'.

Hush Heath Vineyard with world-class facilities.

Pinot Noir grapes from Hattingley Valley Vineyard in Hampshire.

A BRIEF HISTORY OF VINEYARDS IN BRITAIN

Wine has certainly been consumed, if not produced, in the UK since Roman times. From the early medieval era, vineyards were established on the sites of religious institutions, but not limited to these places – in fact, the Domesday Book lists over forty vine-growing locations across Britain during the eleventh century, of which only a dozen were of monastic origin.[2]

Over the centuries, however, vineyards declined and Britain became a country that concentrated its efforts on other crops, as well as the pastoral farming for which our countryside became so recognized right up to the present day. It was not until the 1950s that vineyards started developing in the UK as a commercial entity, with the seed of the industry beginning in the southern counties. By the end of the 1970s, there were over 475 acres of vineyard in England and Wales. By the 1990s, over 2,500 acres were established, with vineyards located as far north as Sheffield. Today, there are over 8,600 acres of vines across England and Wales producing grapes for commercial purposes, and this is set to rise.[3]

And let's not forget those artisan wine makers who, throughout the centuries, have produced wine from their garden or glasshouse-cultivated crops for people to enjoy. The cottage industry of home-grown wine has ticked over nicely throughout all the rises and falls of its bigger 'commercial' brother; and this book is aimed as much at these producers as it is those with a sizeable vineyard.

Entrance to the vineyard at Carlton Towers, Yorkshire.

HOW TO USE THIS BOOK

This is your personal guide on your grape to bottle journey. The first section covers the establishment of vines and successful grape production – including choosing, planting and caring for vines, methods to maximize fruit production and how best to harvest to minimize damage.

The next section looks at the wine-making process – steering the producer through each stage in wine production from the pre-*fermentation* stage; covering the equipment and methods needed, with a few handy tricks of the trade thrown in. Finally, the all-important taste of wines is covered; focusing on what flavours to seek and recognize (and which to avoid) in your final product.

The book concludes with an introduction to the business of wine, covering the cost of production from grape to bottle and finally a personal take by the authors on the notoriously mysterious *terroir* and what it really means to wine makers and consumers today.

The hope of this book is to end up a well-thumbed, well-loved kitchen shelf or winery office tome; a constant companion for what the next harvest will bring.

Winter pruning at Renishaw Hall Vineyard.

CHAPTER 1

GRAPE VARIETIES AND SITE SELECTION

Vines enjoying the glorious weather at Ashling Park, West Sussex.

The classic sparkling wine varieties of Chardonnay, Pinot Noir and Pinot Meunier have captured the imagination with recent plantings in the UK. However, research into what will realistically grow in your vineyard location is of vital importance if your project is to be successful.

OPPOSITE: **Greenhouse-grown Muscat.**

If you are planting vines in the south/south-east of England, with a warm and sheltered site, all of the classic Champagne varieties should successfully ripen, plus varieties like Bacchus, Ortega and Pinot Gris. And, if the weather continues to become more suited to grape growing, then it is likely we will even see more Sauvignon Blanc and Riesling being planted and ripened with confidence in the south of the UK.

Camel Valley Vineyard in Cornwall grows a blend of French and Germanic varieties.

For people looking to grow and ripen those varieties in the midlands or north of England, success is likely to be far harder than if you were looking to grow early ripening varieties. There are, of course, exceptions – for example, Pinot Noir successfully growing in Yorkshire – but if you are seeking a commercially viable crop and tonnage to match, the crop size of these varieties will be significantly smaller. Hence, when growing fruit anywhere that is away from the south-east and southern zones of the UK, it is recommended to go for varieties like Seyval Blanc for sparkling, Rondo and Regent for red, and Solaris and Madeleine Angevine for white wine. These varieties, handled correctly, will yield well and will produce very nice wines: Seyval can produce fruit-driven wines, making it the ideal variety for sparkling wine; Rondo and Regent provide great colour, with hedgerow and blackberry flavours; whilst Solaris and Madeleine can be incredibly diverse, producing fruity Sauvignon Blanc style wines one year and then the next a more mineral flavour.

It is also important to plan your grape varieties with the user in mind. Are you planning to grow grapes solely for commercial reasons, or are these grapes going to be used for wine tailored to you and your taste? What volume are you producing? What proportions of your wine will be red, white or sparkling? These factors will have an impact on the your choice of vines, but, most importantly, what you plant should always be what is best suited to the location and not simply what you would *like* to grow, otherwise you may end up with a vineyard without much fruit.

If producing *traditional-method* sparkling wines, go for varieties that are relatively neutral in flavour with medium to high levels of acidity. These acids provide firm structure that can either soften over time, or will make the ideal vehicle for the secondary fermentation to add *autolytic* flavours (bread, biscuit, brioche, dough).

If you are producing tank-fermented wines or traditional-method wines with less *lees* ageing, the fruitier grapes from the Germanic varieties will be preferable, as you will be less concerned with autolysis and focusing instead on the enhancement of fruit.

When planting vines in cooler parts of the UK the following are recommended choices:

- Seyval Blanc – for the production of sparkling wine, also well suited to barrel ageing
- Reichensteiner – for the production of sparkling wine, but will also produce very nice still wines in warmer years
- Solaris – for production of dry white wine, very disease-resistant and a good cropping varietal
- Madeleine Angevine – for the production of dry white wine, well suited to barrel ageing
- Müller-Thurgau – for the production of a drier white wine

Breaky Bottom Vineyard hidden away in the South Downs growing some of the best grapes for wine in the UK.

- Rondo – for the production of red or rosé wine
- Regent – for the production of red or rosé wine.

Many of these varieties – Seyval Blanc in particular – benefit from being extremely hardy in tougher growing conditions and can be successfully grown almost anywhere in the UK. This fruit can be left on the vine for extended periods of time and it is not uncommon to be harvesting in November.

In slightly warmer locations, the next tranche of varietals include:

- Bacchus – for the production of dry white wine
- Ortega – for the production of dry white wine
- Pinot Noir Précoce – for the production of rosé and red wine.

For a site with guaranteed warmer/sunnier conditions:

- Chardonnay – for the production of sparkling wine and dry white wine
- Pinot Noir – a great all-rounder; could be used for white, red, rosé and sparkling; is *clone*-dependent
- Pinot Blanc – for the production of dry white wine and a good base for sparkling if a marginal site
- Pinot Gris – for the production of dry white wine
- Sauvignon Blanc – for the production of dry white wine; requires an excellent position.

As the weather gets warmer across the country and the planting of more varietals takes place, the crucial thing is still to plant the correct variety for your site.

ROOTSTOCKS AND CLONES

When choosing a vine, it is not simply a matter of selecting a varietal and putting it in the ground. A grapevine comes in two parts, one being the *rootstock* and the other the vine itself. The rootstock's role is to protect the vine from disease, most famously phylloxera – a microscopic louse that lives on and eats the roots of grapevines. This insect decimated vineyards across Europe in the nineteenth century.

Since then, rootstocks have thankfully been adapted to be specifically resistant to this insect and now vines come grafted on to them. However, these rootstocks

Chardonnay vines.

do not come in a 'one size fits all' situation and it is really important to match the rootstock to the soil – a key reason to carry out soil analysis before planting any vines. For example, a vigorous rootstock on a vigorous site is going to give the potential for a vine that is heavy in foliage, creating much work throughout the life cycle of the vine. The same idea goes for a low-vigour rootstock on a low-vigour site – inevitably an even worse scenario, as the vine will not be strong enough to support fruit. Therefore, a match and a balance must be made, specific to soil, climate and topography.

The choice of clone is also of great importance – there are over 1,000 different type of Pinot Noir clones, for example. Some will produce grapes that have tighter bunches with smaller grapes that result in lower yields and higher sugars; these clones are more suitable for red wine production and are associated with the Burgundy region. However, the clones that are most commonly planted in Champagne have larger berries, looser bunches (that result in being more disease-resistant) and lower sugars. Trying to produce red wine from these clones would struggle to be on a par with the Burgundian clones. Some growers will choose to plant a cross section of clones to create greater complexity with the resulting wine, as it is known that each clone has distinctive characteristics.

GROWING METHODS – BIODYNAMIC, ORGANIC OR IPM?

You have chosen your varietals, clone and rootstock; now to consider how you are going to grow your vines. Are you going to grow them traditionally using non-organic chemicals, or are you going to go down an *organic* and/or *biodynamic* route? There are many factors that will influence your decision on what is best for you and your site.

If you are producing small-batch wine from a greenhouse, back garden or allotment, it is possible to have more flexibility as you are clearly not going to be relying on selling the fruit or making the wine as your sole income. If, however, this is to be a venture to earn revenue, you will want to try to achieve more control over all of the possible predicaments that exist and – often – having control through the use of non-organic chemicals may be the better option for your site and your business.

An organic/biodynamic way of producing grapes can be more expensive and is certainly more time-consuming than using non-organic chemicals. If you are using organic sprays, for example, you will have to spray more often in the vineyard than with regular chemicals. It is important to research and weigh up different factors like this, as, if you are opting to have an organic site from a purely environmental perspective, but then are driving up and down the rows more times due to spraying more often, does the increase in diesel outweigh your original motives?

There is scepticism about biodynamic processes, as many of its practices and treatments can appear at times 'mysterious', such as practices linked to lunar cycles. However, it seems to be the case that biodynamic vineyards produce consistently higher-quality fruit than traditional and organic vineyards.

In brief, the father of the biodynamic movement was Rudolf Steiner and through a series of lectures he laid out his philosophy of the farm as a 'living organism' where everything is interconnected, thus any disease that the vine may encounter is an indication of a wider problem with the ecosystem of the entire vineyard and shows that poor practices are occurring in the vineyard as a whole.[4]

Sheep helping to keep the grass down at Blackdown Ridge Vineyard in Sussex.

Biodynamic – like organic – can make use of the same sprays and the only physical difference is the treatments. It has been shown that converting to biodynamics does not require a great deal more work than organic.

Without doubt, the key is to try to do everything we can to help the environment and the soils in the vineyard and to create a space that produces quality grapes, but in a harmonious way. Whatever route you take, you should be spraying minimally and using timings to produce the best possible results – not just applying a thick coat of chemicals. You should also ensure that all sprays are directed where they are needed and not being lost into the atmosphere (more on this below).

Finally, for the organic grape producer, ensure you select as disease-resistant varieties as possible. Grape varieties such as Solaris, Seyval Blanc and Rondo tend to do well with less spraying.

If organic or biodynamic is not really a viable option for your site, the approach you can adopt is *integrated pest management* (IPM). IPM is about being proactive in the vineyard and getting ahead of problems, as opposed to being reactive and using sprays to solve problems as they occur. It is a cultural method that looks at alternatives as much as possible to produce a viable vineyard, so combining the best of organic/ biodynamic with traditional viticulture. IPM covers all aspects of the vineyard's needs and, with timely applications of the correct sprays, this can go a long way to ensuring that your fruit and vineyard are in top condition.

SPRAY APPLICATION

Whatever method of growing vines you opt for, everything in the vineyard has to be about efficiency – so spraying has to be carried out at the correct time and also in the correct way. Nozzles should be checked prior to any spray operation to make sure that they are all working effectively. If you are using a boom sprayer this is especially important, as at the start of the growing season it is not necessary to use all of the nozzles and it is simply a waste of spray, as well as the potential damage being caused to the environment by emitting spray into the atmosphere.

The weather is critical when spraying and conditions need to be dry and calm to get the sprays on to the vine effectively or – again – they run the risk of being lost to the atmosphere. If your vineyard is under an acre in size – and you have the physical strength – then working with a knapsack sprayer means no vehicles and therefore no diesel being used on site; it is certainly a cost-effective way of managing small vineyards.

Before embarking on any spray operation, it is a requirement that you receive full training. In the UK, if you are using a professional pesticide you must hold a valid certificate, or be under the direct supervision of someone who has the certificate. Training is normally a day for the basic course, followed by further days depending on how you are spraying, and covers all of the major points in the vineyard. It's recommended to do the training; it will help to keep both you and the environment within which you are operating safe.

CHAPTER 2

VINEYARD PLANNING

Close-up of nice straight rows at Astley Park Vineyard in Worcestershire.

GROWING DEGREE DAYS

Growing degree days (GDDs) are a useful reference for whether or not an area could be suitable for grape growing, as they allow the vineyard owner to assess his or her site against any wine region in the world and draw a direct comparison. A growing degree day is a simple concept to understand and it is achieved by using the mean temperature of any given day in spring and summer, then subtracting 10°C; this gives the growing degree day figure for that day. For example, if the mean temperature of a day is 15°C minus 10°C, this leaves you with 5°C. If you were to have thirty days in the month at this temperature, there would then be 150 GDDs for the month.

In the UK, we often like to compare our GDDs with other regions and it is certainly interesting, especially when one considers that our GDDs now look very similar to our nearest recognized world-class wine-production region – Champagne. The GDDs in Champagne are between 900 and 1,050; in the UK we

OPPOSITE: Marked-out rows of vines in a grid system, all by hand; attention to detail is the key to success.

are now comfortably in that zone, with the best years touching 1,000 GDDs. This is certainly a very good indicator that the weather is becoming more suitable for grape growing and therefore the sparkling wine varietals associated with Champagne.

As well as comparing European wine regions, it is also interesting to compare other cool climate wine-producing regions to see what can be learnt from their experiences. For many years in the UK, the focus has been on New Zealand and Marlborough specifically. Marlborough has an interesting recent history, as it has come from having practically no wine industry to being a global player; of significance, the region has similar GDDs to the UK. However, it is important to read these figures with caution, as although our temperatures and rainfall levels are broadly similar, New Zealand has far more sunshine hours and far greater ultra-violet penetration than in the UK.

SOIL

One of the great advantages of UK grape growing is the variety of soil types and it is not the case that quality wines can only be made with certain soils, such as chalk, sand or loam. Like all plants, there are some conditions that a vine favours and others that should be avoided, such as heavy clays, shallow soils, poor drainage or high levels of salts for example. However, deep soils with gravel, sand or moderate chalk are ideal conditions for vines to flourish; too highly fertile soils can lead to excessive vegetative growth that may lead to more shade, potentially more disease, more sprays required and ultimately, less quality fruit. There are always exceptions and although the UK has the same band of chalk running through it as has Champagne, currently probably the most lauded of all UK fruit comes from the heavy clay soils of the Essex region.

Before planting any vineyard, it is crucial to get the soil analysed for its qualities – *pH* and nutrient levels – so that the potential of the site can be determined. Often the person planting the vineyard has a set vision of wanting a vineyard on a particular site (quite often by or near their home) and so will plant vines on that site without consideration of whether or not the site can really work; or, at the least, whether it requires any further nutrients or other additions to balance the soils. If the pH values are not too out of balance, it is usually possible to correct these levels; however, if they are very uneven, the pH will have to be corrected at least every four years to ensure that the vineyard remains in good health.

Marking out the vines for a new vineyard on clay soils at Harbour Hills Vineyard near Bromsgrove, Worcestershire.

Once analysis has been carried out, it is advisable to seek the advice of an agronomist to ascertain the strengths and weaknesses of your site as a potential vineyard. If deficiencies are discovered prior to planting, as much as possible should be done to rectify the soil before any vines are put into the ground. Many growers will continue to add fertilizer to strengthen the vines so that they can grow as strongly as possible in

Woodchester Valley Vineyard's terroir near Stroud, Gloucestershire.

Solaris vine with SO4 rootstock planted in Derbyshire – an ideal vine for cool climate wine making.

the first two years prior to any crop being taken. Once the vine is cropping, continued monitoring of the site and its soils is a good idea, allowing you to keep the correct balance of soils for optimum growing.

Vine roots like to go deep into the soil, therefore there needs to be good soil depth that will allow the roots to find moisture and nutrients from lower down. The more established route networks of older vines, where the roots have buried deeply in search of water and nutrients, will often lead to more flavoursome grapes than younger vines that take their water from nearer the surface. Thus, planting on deeper soils will allow vines the chance to search deeper for nutrients within the ground.

TOPOGRAPHY AND LOCATION

Topography is a vital consideration when planning your vineyard. Vines should be planted in the manner that most suits the topographical layout; there is little point trying to shoehorn a south-facing vineyard out of a slope that is dominated in a different direction. Not least, it will lead to dangerous driving conditions for the vineyard operator, with a risk of tractors rolling due to rows being planted in the wrong direction. In regard to the aspect and slope of a vineyard, it is also not advisable to plant in a northerly direction unless it is a very gentle slope, as your site will not get the required sunshine hours to ripen the fruit fully.

In cooler climates, due south is usually the best aspect to plant, as the vine has 100 per cent exposure to the sun throughout the day, from sunrise through to dusk. However, if the topography better suits, it can be advantageous to plant either easterly or westerly; planting in an east-facing direction means that the vines get to dry out earlier in the morning, which may be a positive factor to stave off vineyard problems like mildews and fungal infections. Planting in a west-facing direction can be positive, as the afternoon sun has the greatest heat penetration.

If your vineyard is not totally perfect in its aspect, it is worth thinking about maximizing its position by choosing a grape variety that suits sparkling wine production instead of still wine. If producing sparkling wines, the sugars do not have to be as high as in still wine production, so a potential weakness can be made into a positive.

In cooler climates, it is beneficial if the slope faces the sun at its full height during the day, not least due to allowing more efficient water drainage. Sloping also allows cold air to move away from the vineyard, lessening the risk of frost pockets, which will be more likely in sites where the land is flat.

Latitude can also be considered, although it is not a factor that we can do anything to 'control'. Historically, vineyards across the world have been planted between 30 and 50 degrees, but as the only point in the UK that is this southerly is the southernmost tip of the Lizard Peninsula, this is not something we can achieve in the UK. There is an argument that the nearer one can be to 50 degrees latitude, the higher chance of success one will have at growing vines and ripening fruit. However, with the changes to the weather and growing conditions that are being experienced year on year in the UK, and if the correct varietal and site have been considered, grapes can be grown and ripened much further north than latitude would dictate.

Proximity to the coast will affect how your vines fare. Being close to the coast will decrease the risk of spring frost damage, in the same way that being close to a large body of inland water will carry out the same principle. However, being near the coast may also mean that the temperature will be generally cooler than inland. Coastal sites can also experience warm, wet maritime weather systems that are an ideal haven for fungal disease amongst the vines. Therefore, there is a lot to consider with coastal sites and ultimately what will dictate your decision will be the local conditions.

Wind chill has a massive effect on a vineyard, which is why a small, sheltered vineyard will often produce higher quality fruit than a more exposed vineyard. Warm, sheltered conditions are ideal for grapevines. For those planting on a larger scale armed with this knowledge, it is possible to plant vines in such a way that protects different parts of the vineyard, with the more prized grapes coming from a position of shelter. Ideally, your location should be as calm and as benign as possible in regard to wind conditions. The greater the wind, the cooler the site and, at this stage, UK viticulture cannot deliberately embark on trying to create cool conditions in which to grow fruit – although this may change.

Altitude of any potential site also needs to be taken into consideration. Mean temperature decreases by approximately 0.6°C per 100m above mean sea level and anything over 100m would not be considered an ideal vineyard location in the UK. However, it is possible to plant a vineyard above 100m, but the varieties would need to suit these cooler conditions.

To be successful at growing fruit in a cool climate the three factors of temperature, rainfall and sunshine hours are the ones to really care about. There are areas of East Anglia, for instance, that are considered the best place to grow fruit in the UK, yet these areas are many miles from the most southerly areas of the UK which, overall, experience warmer weather. It would seem that a dry location with long sunshine hours is of upmost importance.

Rows capture all the summer sun at Harbour Hills vineyard.

CULTIVATION

Cultivation in a cool climate is an interesting subject as so many of the vineyards in the rest of the world are planted and kept on land free from pests and plants. A lot changed when cool climate wines started to be produced in places like Tasmania and New Zealand and their research allowed many cool climate regions like the UK to catch up rapidly. The knowledge gained meant that we could understand how best to use cultivation – or not – to get the best out of our vines. In a wet climate, for example, allowing some competition can be a positive thing, as the grasses and other plants growing alongside the vine draw away excess water. However, when planting and establishing a vineyard it can be seen as best practice to cultivate to avoid other crops so as to keep the majority of the nutrients and water for the establishing vine.

Bare earth also allows for greater heat accumulation over the season, which can lead to riper fruit with more condensed flavours in the finished wine. Additionally, with no cover crop the risk of frost is also reduced, as cold air will more easily drain away from the vineyard. As per all practices in the vineyard, there is a balance to be had; too much cultivation can lead to soil erosion that damages the soil and decreases the productivity of the vines and will result in water run-off that may direct wanted nutrients away from the vines. Humidity can also play a part; by having bare earth it will mean that the vineyard is less humid, which will in turn lead to fewer incidences of fungal issues amongst the grapes.

However, taking another perspective, a cover crop can be viewed as a positive thing, as the vines will need to work harder to seek moisture and will therefore go deeper into the soil, which should result in more interesting wines in the process.

It is also often visually more appealing to see a vineyard that has well-maintained grass or cover crops. As any small producer knows, your number one sales tool is the vineyard itself, so the look and ambience will be amongst the main considerations.

A workable option can be to cultivate every other row, which benefits both the soil and the vines. It aids and increases nitrogen levels and gives the vines less competition, while still allowing competition on the adjacent row. The following year, the untouched row can then be ploughed, with grass allowed to retake the ploughed row. It also allows the opportunity to experiment with other types of cover crops that are beneficial to the soils.

Gently south-facing slopes at Blackdown Ridge Vineyard.

PRACTICAL CONSIDERATIONS

Layout and Trellis System

So, what is the best layout for your site? Again, so much of this is down to the topography of the area where you will be growing your vines, although there are some factors that will be relevant across all situations.

Straight Rows

If you are planting a small vineyard by hand, you will need rope or twine to mark out where your vines are going to go, and you must ensure that everything is straight. Never plant by eye – it is practically impossible to plant in a straight line this way.

Ensure that you have plenty of rope/twine for straight rows and grids – never plant by eye.

Avoid Shade

Never encourage shading in the vineyard. The row width minimums should be linked to the height of your trellis systems. It is fairly standard practice to make widths at least 180–200cm wide and for the complete height of the trellis to match. A consideration for the width of the vineyard will also be what equipment and machinery you will be using to manage the site. If you

Trellis height should not be greater than row width, or it will create shade in the canopy – Carlton Towers Vineyard, Yorkshire.

are planting a small vineyard on your farm, for instance, and all of your machinery is over 2m wide, planting tight rows would make little sense – the row widths should be matched to the machinery you are using. Also ensure that you leave plenty of turning space at the end of the rows so that your vehicle and anything it is towing can easily traverse between rows. If you are planting vines in an allotment or garden, you will have greater flexibility as to the layout and row widths.

The focus for vine trellising in this book is vertical shoot positioning (VSP). It is my experience that VSP on the average cool climate soils in the UK will provide the vine and the canopy with enough sunlight and warmth to ripen fruit year on year. It is true that a successful trellis system should be in balance, so that there is neither too much vegetative growth nor too little. The same applies to fruit production – if too many bunches are left to ripen it will lead to a decrease in quality of fruit. Balance is the key word; shade in the canopy leads to a decrease in quality of grapes that are higher in acid, more prone to disease, more herbaceous tasting and lower in sugars. Therefore, every effort should be made to open up the canopy and increase the sunlight, warmth and airflow within the area surrounding the fruiting zone.

It is recommended in the first instance to plan for a vineyard that will become VSP double *guyot* (two fruiting arms), but whilst it is establishing it should be pruned in such a way as to be single guyot (one fruiting arm). Once established from single guyot, if there is excessive vegetative growth it is straightforward to convert to double guyot. If there is still excessive growth, it is then possible to convert your vineyard to other systems, such as the Scott Henry training system or the Te Kauwhata Two Tier (TK2T) system developed by Dr Richard Smart. These systems create the conditions for greater yield and higher quality if your site is producing excessive growth with VSP double guyot as they lead to more fruiting arms on the vine and therefore more buds.[5]

Space between Vines

This will be dictated by planting systems, with the aim of having no crossover of the vines' fruiting arms, as this leads to shade in the canopy and fruit of a lower potential quality. Shade can also lead to more chance of mildews and unwanted fungal disease due to the cooler temperatures and lack of wind flow. Vine spacing can also manage vigour and will have an influence on the end tonnage, sugars and acids of the grapes. The optimal vine spacing would be linked to the fertility of the rootstock, vine type, weather and the grape varietal planted.

Fruiting Wire

This should be installed 80–100cm off the ground. If you are on a vigorous and warm site 100cm may be more suitable, as there may come a time when you will want to switch your trellis system and grow extra fruiting arms to maximize growth and fruit production. If you do this, it is possible to train fruiting arms up and down, to get more *nodes* and therefore more potential fruit (Scott Henry system).

Other Wires

These are put in place during installation to catch the shoots as they grow from the nodes. There is not a definitive ideal distance to place these wires; however, being equidistant from the fruiting wire would be the most logical layout. For example, if your fruiting wire is set at 100cm, the next pair of wires should be 35cm, followed by a further set 35cm higher at 170cm from the ground. These wires should be set in place so that they can be moved throughout the season, as this makes tucking in easier.

Posts

It is highly recommended to use stainless-steel posts, as they will weather far better than wooden posts.

Stainless-steel posts are highly recommended as wooden posts will degrade.

Wooden posts will have a life of approximately a decade before they become too wet and start to fail due to the constant tension on the wood from the wires, as the wood is repeatedly shifting between wet and dry.

Hand-Planting a Vineyard

Below is a list of the basic equipment required for hand-planting a vineyard:

- **Tape measure** This is used to measure out the rows and to show where the vines are going to be planted.
- **Rope/twine/string** These are needed to mark out the rows and grids physically so that you know where the rows are going, but also where the vines are being placed. By producing a grid (this does not have to be across the whole vineyard – that would be a huge task!), you are ensuring that the

vines are square to each other and that the rows are as straight as possible.

- **Shovel/auger** If you have a bigger budget, an auger can be a great bit of kit to use for planting vines. However, a shovel works equally well; it just requires more effort to produce a hole big enough in which to put the vine (ensure that the roots have enough space to grow down).
- **Post basher** You need a post basher to put the end posts and intermediate posts into the ground. Be sure to get these posts in deep, as they are going to be in the ground for a considerable amount of time. However, do not go in too deep as you need to ensure that the wires are going to be at the correct height to support the vines.
- **Wire and accessories** Always use good quality vineyard wire, between 2–2.5mm in thickness. Make sure that any tensioning kit matches your choice of wire.
- **Ground anchors** Anchoring the end posts needs to be taken into consideration. Use an anchoring system to make life easier.
- **Vine guards** These effectively act as small polytunnels for the vine and are crucial in bringing on development in the first couple of seasons of a vine's establishment. However, be aware that these guards are also a haven for unwanted mildews and infections, due to the warmth created by these small areas. The guards can also attract snails and so should be checked regularly to ensure that the vines are the only living things within – popping slug and snail repellent inside each guard can be effective. Guards should stay on a vine until it is strong enough for fruiting arms to be selected – normally the end of the second growing season.
- **Canes/stakes** These are used to support the vine. Metal stakes are a good idea, as bamboo canes tend to break easily and are havens for bugs. These stakes also double up as markers if you are going to set up your vineyard in grids to ensure that you achieve straight lines.
- **Vine ties** These ensure that the vine stays secure to its support. Make sure that the ties can stretch, however, to avoid causing damage by the girdle as the vine grows.

For larger sites, the only major difference in tools or equipment required would be how the vines are put into the ground. This would take the form of GPS-guided machinery to plant the vines – for a larger site this would be a far more cost-effective approach and much faster.

TRELLIS SYSTEM

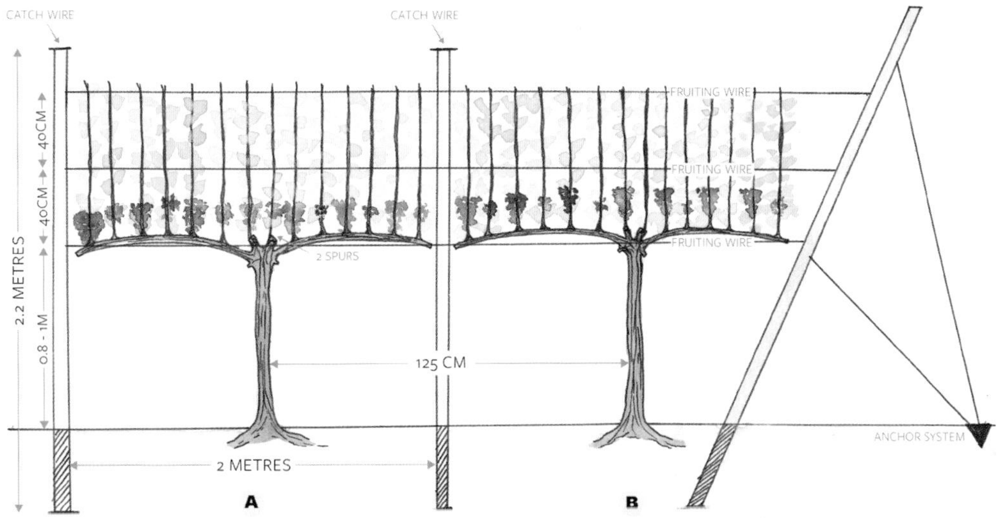

Trellis system – showing recommended distances for double guyot and vertical shoot positioning.

Checklist

This checklist is by no means exhaustive, but the following actions should be carried out before planting your vines:

- **Order your vines in good time** – at least twelve months ahead of the proposed plant date and the wholesalers will deliver the vines when you need them. Many of the desirable grape varietals for the UK get fully booked up, so earlier is better to avoid disappointment. Remember that it is important to know what rootstock and clone are the ideal type for the style of wine you want to produce, but also that the type can work on your site.
- **Equipment** – if you do not own it, plan and book the equipment required to plant, for example tractors/ploughs if a larger site, or rotavator if smaller.
- **Pests** – if you have existing pests, come up with a plan to stop them from eating your vines and order appropriate preventative measures.
- **Vine guards and stakes** – order a vine guard and stake for every vine, plus a few additional ones in case of breakage.
- **Wire** – work out the length of the vineyard, then buy enough wire for the fruit wire plus 4× tucking-in wires. So if your vineyard row is 20m long, you will need 100m worth of wire per row, plus wire for anchoring. As a rule, add a further 10 per cent to allow for anchoring and to allow for extra requirements.
- **Posts** – you will require two end posts plus a post every five vines.
- **Wire connectors/tensioners** – allow for twelve per row as minimum.

LAND PREPARATION

Before planting any vines, you will need to have prepped the land. Many commercial sites will completely weed-kill the whole site prior to planting; however, this can be seen as an unfavourable option for the soil itself, as everything has been killed off. I prefer to remove all grass and competition firstly by deep ploughing, followed by power-harrowing the site. This removes competition for the vines while not destroying the seeds, so that the grasses that were originally there will grow back with time. If you choose to use weedkiller to kill the grass, seed-drill a cover crop afterwards, or else the resulting space will soon become full of unwanted plants like stinging nettles, thistles and brambles that become extremely difficult to remove once established.

Newly planted Pinot Noir vine and cane.

Once the vineyard site has been ploughed and power-harrowed, the soil should be easy to work with and to plant. Do not over-harrow the site; you are not trying to achieve a powdery finish.

PLANTING

Buy vines from an accredited dealer; these vines will come in packs of twenty-five. Any preparation of the vines should be at the direction of the person selling them, as it is possible that the vines will have been prepared already for direct planting. If no direction is given, it is standard practice to do the following. First, the vine roots should be trimmed to the size of a large fist grip (8cm). Next, the vines should be left to soak in water prior to going in the ground. It is also recommended to dip the vines in a solution that encourages *mycorrhizal* development, so that the vines get the best possible chance to flourish.

When digging a hole, it should be deep enough and wide enough for the vine to sit in comfortably and for the top of vine (the element that has been grafted) to sit clearly above ground. The hole should then be filled in with the roots facing downward and watered well – do ensure that the roots are pointing straight down or it can cause the roots to grow upward, which ultimately will affect the long-term health of the vine. It may even cause a 'J-root', which will not allow your vine to flourish. Once in the ground, a stake should be placed near the vine (a few cm) and a vine guard be placed around the stake and vine.

There are different ways of growing a young vine and these are covered in more detail in Chapter 3. In year one, it is best to let the vine grow and the two strongest shoots should be encouraged with the others removed. Most importantly, ensure that the vine does not have any competition and if any flowers are produced by the vine, they should be removed immediately.

In year two, the vine should be pruned back to the two strongest buds from the nearest point above the graft and allowed to grow. Once it is obvious which of the two strongest buds is producing the strongest shoot, the weakest can be pruned off, allowing the strongest shoot to grow and be gently tied to the stake so that the growth is vertical. Make sure that whatever you use to tie the vine to the stake will not girdle the vine as it grows. This shoot should have the capacity to grow in excess of 1.8m if so desired, but it can be pruned to 1.8m if not. Again, if any flowering occurs, this should be removed to put growth into the strength of the vine and not into fruit production.

In year three, the vine can either be pruned to just below the fruit wire to the nearest bud, or it can be bent over to form what would become the start of a single guyot trellis system. The decision of whether to bend the shoot over or to prune should be carried out based on the strength of the vine below the fruiting wire. If comfortably thicker than a finger width, then starting the trellis is possible. If weaker, pruning to the fruiting wire is the better option. Whatever option you choose, ensure that two spurs are left at the top of the crown for the following year. This is crucial to all pruning, to ensure that the vine always grows from the area of the crown.

Prepping Pinot Noir vines before planting – roots trimmed and soaked in water for 24 hours.

OTHER CONSIDERATIONS

Make sure that unwanted buds on the trunk are removed at the earliest possible opportunity. If using *herbicide*, spray whilst the vine is dormant, as the sprays can kill the vine if they come into contact with any leaf. Also ensure that a spray programme is put in place to stop any unwanted mildews or fungal infections. This should be done in the first year and carried on, and not only from the first year of fruit, as many of the fungal diseases will over-winter on vines.

The author planting vines by hand, using plenty of rope to mark the rows.

CHAPTER 3

GROWING VINES

HOW TO CARE FOR THE VINE: YEARS ONE TO THREE

So your vines are now in the ground – what do you do next? The first few years of vine growth is a period in which many basic errors can occur, mostly because people understandably are eager to see fruit as soon as possible.

Remove Any Competition

It is crucial that the area around your vines is kept clear of competing plants and these should be removed as soon as they are seen. Remove at least 30cm of competition in all directions from the vine; this does include grass. Very often too much grass is left near the vines in the first year and all growth will compete with the vine. You should also ensure that snails are not inside grow tubes, as they will eat the leaves on young vines.

To establish the vines successfully, treat a one-year-old vine in the same way that you would a more mature vine and spray as applicable to stop fungal spores developing on the vine. If you have a small number of vines, this can be carried out with a hand-held sprayer; for a larger site, use a backpack.

Remember, what you see above the ground is replicated below the ground – in other words, if you have a weak-looking vine above ground, it is likely that the roots below are also weak.

OPPOSITE: **Rondo grapes pre-veraison.**

Pruning and Establishing the Vine

From Zero to Twelve Months

If the vines were planted in April, by midsummer they should be pruned back to the two strongest shoots at the most, and at the least do nothing at all.

After Ten Months

You now need to prune back to the two strongest buds at the base – or near the base – of the vine. Ensure that you prune above the graft, thus giving the vine the greatest opportunity to become stronger and to support its longevity. These two strongest shoots should be encouraged to grow and once you have one shoot that is clearly stronger than the other, the weaker shoot can be pruned off. The remaining shoot and its leaves should be sprayed ongoing as part of the vineyard spray programme, so that fungal disease is not allowed to take a grip on the vine.

If your vine has any sign of flowering throughout the establishment phase, the flowers should be removed immediately so that energy is not being used up in fruit production.

After Twenty Months

Following the end of the vine's second season, prune back to the two strongest nodes nearest the fruiting wire, again ensuring that the vine has little or no competition and allowing it the best possible opportunity to develop. The shoots will grow happily and strongly from these two nodes and if flowers develop, you can now have a mini-harvest – there is no need to remove any flowering this year.

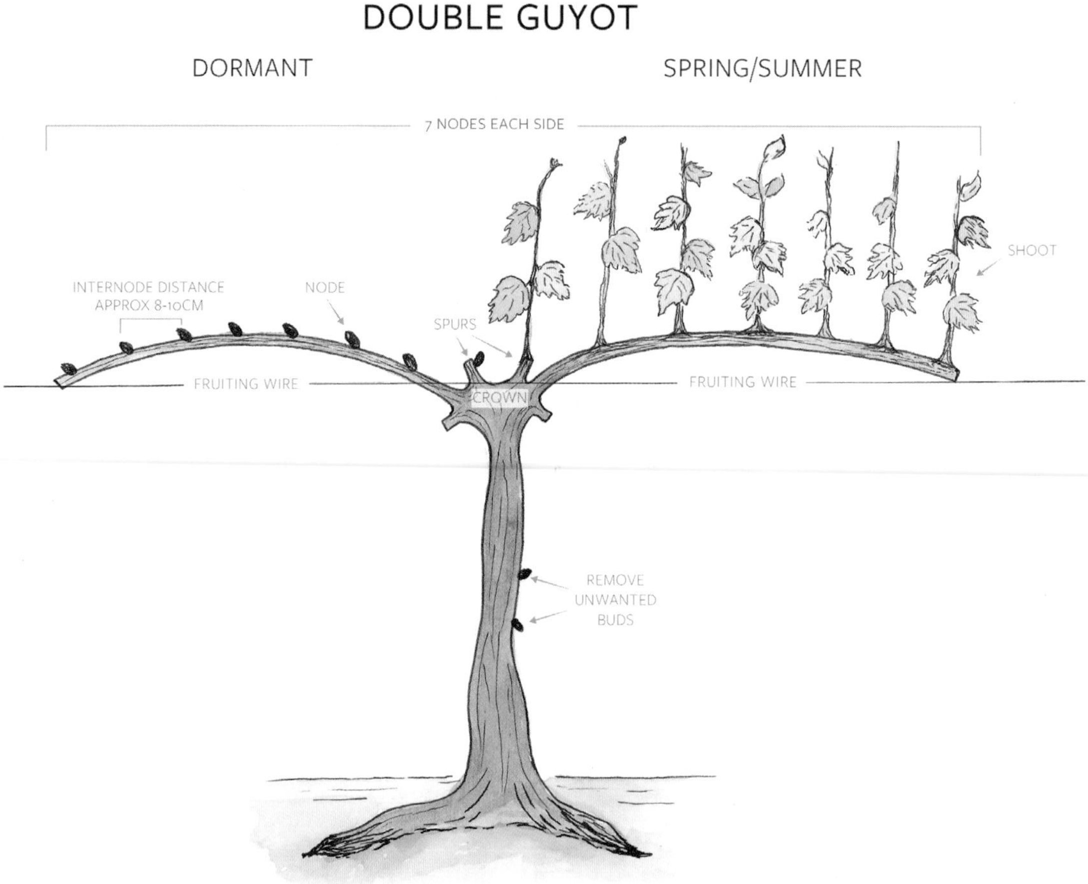

Illustration of the double guyot and VSP trellis system.

Young vine growing in the early summer – note the removal of the competition from around the vine.

After twenty-four months in the ground, the vine is ready to have the fruiting arm tied down.

You should now have the start of what looks like an established vine, with a trunk, the start of a crown and two strong shoots coming from that crown.

After Twenty-Four Months

Following this season, you are now headed into the first year where you are starting the process of tying fruiting arms down.

The fruiting arm should have six or seven nodes and two spurs from the crown. The spurs are in many ways more important than the fruiting arm, as they will ensure that you get shoots growing in the right place for the following season. If you do not leave spurs, it causes crowding in the vine's canopy. The vine is always at its strongest from its furthest point, known as the 'end-point principle'.

During the Third Year

During the third year, operate a single guyot system of six to seven nodes and two spurs per vine. If all is going well, your internode distance should be approximately one fist-width in size. If it is much smaller, you are trying to get too much out of the vine too soon. You should revert to the end of year two of the establishment phase and ensure that the vine has received enough nutrients. If the node length is longer and thicker, you can increase your progress and employ a double guyot system more rapidly.

Single guyot fruiting arm tied down on young vines.

Following Year Three

Your vine should now be on a standard growth cycle where the spurs on the crown supply the fruiting arms for the following year. Do not be tempted to leave too many nodes as an insurance policy, as this will cause crowding at the crown; keep to two only. Add nutrient as applicable to keep your vines happy.

Lighting bougies at Albury Organic Vineyard – bougies increase air temperature in the vineyard, preventing frost damage of young buds and shoots.

Vine-Establishment: Difficulties

There are a number of problems that you may encounter when establishing your vines and it is wise to plan for all of them, even if hopefully not many of them will actually occur. If caught in time, it is possible to avoid these issues greatly affecting your vines.

Frost damage to a young shoot from a late May frost.

Frosts

In the establishment phase, a serious frost may put you back twelve months. Ensure that you plant your vines well into spring, to try to avoid frosts that could kill off buds that have grown early in the season. It is most likely that any frost would not completely kill the vine – just the growth – so, although frustrating, frost should only affect the growth for this year.

Drought

A very dry spring and early summer can also be a big risk factor. It is important to keep vines well watered during the establishment phase, as they require a lot of water to flourish and grow. A regular watering plan should be put in place during any prolonged period of drought. Once your vines are established (and presuming you have planted in a cool climate where there is usually plenty of rain), there should be sufficient water to hydrate the vines throughout the seasons.

Rabbits, Deer and Badgers

If there is anything on your site that may want to eat your vines, you should do your best to remove them from the equation. One of the issues is that if you remove the grass that they normally eat, then the next best option for animals like rabbits will be the vines. Rabbits can often be deterred by vine guards and by giving them alternative food to eat while the vines establish.

As deer is a much larger animal, fencing is a very effective way of keeping them away from the vines. Badgers can be a bit trickier, but they often leave a distinctive trail, which should be blocked and diverted so that they go in a different direction.

Fungal Diseases

Put together a comprehensive spray programme and get advice from your local agricultural vineyard spray specialist. They will often provide free advice on the presumption that you will be buying from them. It is worth noting here that by spraying against fungal diseases it does not mean that you cannot operate an organic vineyard if you so wish. Copper and sulphur sprays are organic and can be an effective way to deal with downy mildew and powdery mildew, although you will most likely have to spray more often.

Fungal disease amongst the grapes.

Pruning Methods: Cane or Spur?

There are two main methods of pruning in the vineyard – *cane* and *spur pruning.*

Cane Pruning

Cane pruning involves taking the previous year's shoots that have grown from the spurs left on the crown from the year before and tying them down on the fruiting wire. Single arm is known as single guyot and double arm is known as double guyot.

All of the previous year's wood – apart from these two shoots that have now lignified (become rigid and woody) and two spurs – should be removed from the vine. These should be the two strongest canes from the crown, with even internode lengths of around 8cm (adult-sized fist).

The strength and voracity of these canes will decide whether a single or double guyot trellis system should be used. It is advisable to base this decision on the strength of the vine and this can be judged by the

Discussing pruning options – cane or spur prune?

Professional pruning teams working at a tremendous speed.

weight of wood that exists within the canopy in the dormant season. When pruning the vine, count every cane that is removed – this is called a 'charge count'. For every cane that is the thickness of a pencil, this would be counted as one. If the cane is twice the diameter of a pencil, this would be two and so on. The length of these canes should be at least 1m long. If the count gives you a figure of between greater than seven and less than fourteen, you should be operating a single guyot system with seven nodes. If the count is fourteen plus, you should be operating a double guyot system of seven nodes on two arms. If the count is over twenty, you should be considering changing your trellis system to accommodate more nodes.

When cane pruning, there is less opportunity for fungal disease because the cane is only allowed to bear fruit for one season before it is removed and another fruiting cane put in its place. It is also thought that the younger wood can bring about more fruitful grapes. As the growing seasons are inconsistent in

A large pile of prunings after a day amongst the vines.

the UK, it allows there to be greater flexibility in what you tie down and, consequently, this approach to UK viticulture is often considered the most appropriate.

Some growers like to keep four fruiting arms not tied down until the last safe moment; this in theory will keep the fruiting arms away from damaging frosts as they are higher off the ground. Once the frost episode has passed, the two arms can be tied down to form double guyot whilst the remaining shoots can be pruned to become the spurs for the next season.

Spur Pruning

Spur pruning is still a popular method, not least because it is very easy to teach and difficult to get wrong. Spur pruning requires there to be a permanent fruiting arm. Each year, you cut back to two buds per spur. This system means that the only thing to ensure is that you do not cut off the buds, or it will result in poor growth. This system is used often in warmer climates less susceptible to mildew, as the wood can overwinter for seasons with fewer problems.

Whatever system you employ, it is always best to prune with the following considerations in mind:

- Large pruning wounds leave a possible gateway for disease into the vine and should be avoided as much as possible. It is also recommended to prune when the sap is rising, so that the sap can help to heal the wound as it happens; this also helps to halt any ingress of disease.
- Any wound on the vine will cause dieback on the vine by around 1.5 times the size of the cut, therefore any pruning cuts should be made with this in mind so that some wood is left as a buffer. This dieback can halt the progress of the sap and can cause areas of the vine to die, which will result in a less fruitful vine.
- It is best practice to take fruiting arms from the opposite side of the crown for double guyot as far as possible, to encourage sap flow throughout the vine. If growing for single guyot, adopt the same approach with the spur.

VINE MANAGEMENT YEARLY CYCLE, FROM THREE YEARS PLUS

January to March

The vine should be pruned in a style as described above.

When to tie the vines down can be a contested area of discussion. Some vineyards like to tie their

Snow amongst the vines during winter at Polgoon Vineyard in Cornwall – a cold, dormant period can be good for the health of the vines.

Young vine pruning, making the cut just below the fruiting wire.

when eventually tied down, half of them could end up being knocked off. In the UK, the start of April is usually a suitable time to tie down.

Pruning is recommended to be as late as possible in order to give the vines the longest possible time in dormancy before starting the process again, and that sap flow will help to stop the ingress of disease through pruning wounds.

Prune last the parts of your vineyard that are most prone to frost. This should increase the chance of surviving frost episodes by delaying *budburst*

Keeping the best of the pruned vines as cuttings to replant and fill in the gaps in the vineyard.

vines down after the risk of frost has passed, on the understanding that the frost has to be especially severe to affect all of the vines as they remain in a higher position. A warning if doing this, however; if left too late, the buds may have developed to the point that

Makeshift vine-burning barrow – also handy for cooking baked potatoes in the vineyard.

Pruning is probably the most important of all vineyard jobs, as selecting the right shoots to keep or remove decides not only crop weight, but can have a direct correlation with longer-term vine health.

and minimizing the risk to young buds, as they are especially vulnerable to frost during this critical moment in the growing season.

This time also provides an opportunity to fix any trellising and make improvements to the systems that are in place in the vineyard. It is not unusual for end posts to have collapsed if they are made of wood, so this is a job for the dormant season. It is always recommended to use metal posts as wooden posts have a short shelf life, due to wet weather and the strain of wires and vines.

Take the opportunity at the end of March also to fix any nutrient issues in the vines by adding a ready-mixed formula, following a soil analysis, to tackle any nutrient deficiencies. Signs of a nutrient-deficient vine include short internode length and weak growth. Improving nutrient levels of soil can be carried out with a granular spreader or equivalent. It is also a time to apply weedkiller if using it and to ensure that any shrubs are removed, as it is not uncommon for small trees to start to become established amongst the vines.

Count any gaps amongst the vines and order replacement vines according to your requirements. When counting any gaps, it is good practice to see if there are any patterns to where you are losing vines. This process will allow you to see if there are diseases amongst your vines that can be stopped in their tracks, by taking positive action and removing any sick vines that may be spreading fungal disease.

April to June

April

Budburst, which usually takes place in April, is the most magical time of the year, as the long dormancy ends and life returns to the vines. It is also the time of the year fraught with the most danger, as a frost at this time will decimate your harvest figures and could render the rest of the summer a disappointment.

Bud-rubbing takes place where any unwanted buds that appear mostly on the trunk of the vine should be removed. If left, these buds will become shoots that will sap energy and growth from where you want it on the vine and will also create shade and make operating between rows difficult.

This is a critical period for the success of the vine. If frost is forecast, there are a number of different options to take. These range from lighting small fires using bougies, to trying to disrupt the airflow in the vineyard in order to move the cold air. The latter could be carried

End of April and the start of May will see budburst in the vineyard.

Pre bud-rubbed vine.

Post bud-rubbed vine – timing is crucial to save a lot of effort later in the season.

out with air blowers, or, in some vineyards, cattle are used to bring some heat into small known frost-pocketed areas. Often, however, the threat of a late frost is a time when you just have to cross everything and hope for the best.

If a late frost does occur, the first thing you will notice is that the leaves will curl and appear burnt. The frost will lead to a loss in yield and how severe will depend upon your vineyard site. If your site is prone to late-season frosts, it would be best practice to keep two to three times the number of canes per vine when you prune, then quickly remove the extra canes after the final frost opportunity has passed so that your vine is back in balance; this will give you the highest chance of a crop from the remaining unaffected buds.

May

After budburst, you will start to see the growth of *inflorescence* on the vines. Inflorescence looks like the formation of tiny bunches of grapes, but what is below the caps that are formed are not grapes, but flowers.

Following budburst, we have inflorescence – beneath the cap are the precious flowers and the formation of fruit.

As the cap falls, the young flowers and the infant grape are exposed.

These flowers are a crucial stage, which will dictate the quality of the fruit that the vines should yield.

Rain at this time of the year will often set the conditions for the quality of grapes. If the flowers become damaged due to heavy rain or the caps become stuck, this will usually mean a poor fruit set. Unfortunately, there is not a lot that you can do about this, unless you plant in polytunnels. With your spray programme in place, the first sprays should now be on the vine.

June

As the shoots begin to grow vertically, make sure that the vines are growing inside the trellis system and that all the shoots are growing in the desired direction so that they do not expand out into the rows. This will require some well-directed tucking in of the vines. If you have movable foliage wires, now is the time to get them in place as the vines start to grow within the trellis.

Young shoot with inflorescence growing in the canopy.

July to September

Once flowering has passed, you will start to notice the formation of fruit and grapes appearing from where the flowers were. At this stage, and not before, you should consider hedging operations, usually around the end of June. Hedging is the trimming of the vines at the top of the catch wires and of any shoots that may be growing out into the rows. Be mindful not to do this too brutally – ensure that enough nodes remain on any of the canes that are coming from the area of the crown, so that fruiting arms will be in place for next year.

Any laterals that have no fruit on can also be removed at this stage; this is a process known as shoot thinning. It has been shown that removing laterals increases the quality of fruit due to less carbohydrates being used for growth of unwanted laterals and less shading in the canopy. Shade can also be decreased in the canopy through leaf stripping. Leaf stripping is the removal of the leaves around the fruiting zone, which will increase airflow and decrease disease at the same time.

Exposing the fruit to sunlight has a massive impact on its quality and causes a drop in acidity and especially a drop in malic acid. Malic acid is the predominant acid that is in green apple, thus by reducing malic acid it will help the juice and in turn the wine will taste softer. In a cool climate you can expose the fruit almost in its entirety, as the chances that the grapes will get sunburnt are remote. However, if you do have an especially hotspot area of your vineyard, achieving dappled sunlight within the canopy and onto the fruit is ideal. Ultimately, this process will come down to your comprehension of the environment within which you are growing your fruit.[6]

As the summer months progress, your fruit will ripen and if you are growing red grapes they will go through a process called *veraison* – the grapes changing colour from green to red. If you are growing white grapes, these will also change colour and will move from green to yellow (depending on the variety) and it will be possible to see the grape starting to plump up and soften. During summer it will be necessary to keep de-leafing and to hedge where appropriate.

Vineyard tractor mowing in the vines to keep the grass down at Little Wold Vineyard.

Leaf stripping to expose the fruit to sunlight to decrease malic acid and raise the quality of the fruit.

Rondo grapes pre-veraison at Renishaw Hall Vineyard in Derbyshire.

Veraison occurring in Pinot Noir grapes.

September and October

As the end of August approaches, harvest will not be too far away for many sites and it is the ideal time to know exactly how your fruit is developing. You can do this with a couple of easy to use tools. The *refractometer* is the easiest to use and will give you a snapshot of the sugar content of the fruit, allowing you to pick based on sugar levels. If you combine this tool with an acid-testing kit, you will have a good indication of when you should be picking the fruit.

Refractometer used in the vineyard to take a snapshot of the sugars in the grapes.

Ideal Sugar and Acid Levels at Harvest

Wine Type	White Wine (Ideal)	Red Wine (Ideal)	Sparkling Wine (Ideal)
Sugars (*potential alcohol* by volume [ABV])	10.5–12%	11–13%+ (max. 15%)	9.5–11.5%
Total acidity (TA)	6–8TA	6–8TA	7.5–11TA

Growers can be very eager to pick the fruit as soon as it seems ready, as so much can go wrong throughout the season. An eye has to be kept on the weather as harvest approaches – picking grapes in the rain is not desirable as it will dilute the juice. Also, the warm, wet conditions that often occur in September are a haven for unwanted fungal disease, which, if it develops near the harvest, cannot be dealt with through chemical means as it will be too late. However, if the fruit is in good shape you will reap the benefits from being patient. Do not pick too soon, unless you have a good reason to (such as you want to blend more acidic juice with riper juice). When the weather gets cooler, although sugars will not rise greatly, acids are still dropping away at a good rate, so if your fruit is not ideal in both parameters, try to get your juice in the ideal category for one parameter. The longer the fruit is left on the vine, the greater *phenolic ripeness* will be achieved and the more delicious your end product.

Ripe fruit ready for the press.

INDOOR-GROWN GRAPEVINES

Whether you have inherited an existing vine growing in a greenhouse in the garden, or are thinking of cultivating your own home-grown grapes for eating or to make wine, vines grown in protected environments tend to flourish and are an enjoyable addition to gardens. Indoor-grown vines do, however, require a little different treatment to vines planted outside.

Popularity

Indoor-grown vines have been a popular horticultural pastime in the UK for hundreds of years. During the late eighteenth and nineteenth centuries, many of the glasshouses located in the private gardens of great estates across the country would have been filled with vines. The anticipation of the deliciously sweet taste of dessert grapes enhanced their popularity as a fruit to cultivate and, if the structures allowed, glasshouses would often house several varieties under one roof, providing an assortment of black and white grapes for the more privileged families across the country.

Today, some of the country's most iconic gardens still yield crops from original vines that are centuries old, the most famous example being the Great Vine

Pickers gearing up for harvest in the greenhouse at Renishaw Hall, Derbyshire.

at Hampton Court Palace. Over 250 years old, it was planted under the instructions of the celebrated landscape gardener, Lancelot 'Capability' Brown. The Great Vine grape variety is Black Hamburg and – along with several other popular varieties for glasshouses or greenhouses – it was grown for eating. Black Hamburg is still a popular grape variety today, not least due to its relative ease to maintain and for producing sweet and attractive-looking grapes. What is not to like about the look of the deep purple grapes adorning a fruit bowl, accompanying a cheeseboard, or forming a splendid centrepiece at a dinner party?

Greenhouse Grape Varieties

Indoor grapes can cater both for eating and for wine making, depending on the volume and variety. With the right care, almost any grape can be successfully grown in an indoor environment. These are some of the more commonly indoor-grown varieties to be found in non-commercial sites across the UK:

- Black Hamburg – high sugar, delicious-tasting grape with a fantastic aroma
- Muscat – dessert grape that thrives in greenhouses, wonderful fruit salad aroma and taste
- Dornfelder – heavy cropping red grape, lovely flavours of hedgerow and bramble fruits
- Bacchus – white grape that thrives in a greenhouse environment, flavours of gooseberry and English hedgerow.

Establishing a Vine in a Greenhouse or Protected Environment

If you are starting from scratch cultivating a vine within a greenhouse, you first need to select the best method of planting to suit your situation. Vines can be grown in containers from inside the greenhouse like many other greenhouse plants. They can also be placed in the earth either inside or outside the structure and the vine trained to grow up inside the greenhouse to benefit from the warm atmosphere, whilst retaining the direct contact with the soil below.

Going for the latter option undoubtedly means more work upfront, modifying the greenhouse or building and successfully training the vine to grow up and inside the building (in fact, it is not uncommon to take down and rebuild a greenhouse structure over an existing, well-established vine as it gets larger). However, this method does normally make the ongoing upkeep of the vine a lot less laborious in the long term, as vines growing directly in the earth will not require as much regular watering, nor the feeding that vines planted in containers inside will need. Grapevines will train well along the inside of a greenhouse, but make sure that you allow plenty of room for each vine. A small greenhouse should only really house one vine.

It is also really important that the greenhouse or building is well ventilated, as well as warm and dry. Grapes are more likely to pick up fungal diseases in a greenhouse that is humid, therefore keep windows and vents partially open during the summer and autumn to lessen this risk. Ensure that vines are watered frequently

First leaf unfurling on a greenhouse vine at Polgoon Vineyard, Cornwall.

during the growing season, especially if grown in pots, and feed with a fertilizer from spring.

Pruning

As with outdoor-grown vines, pruning is key and new growth should be cut right back when the vine is dormant, to allow for the continuing strength of the plant and a good crop. Vines growing from the ground and into the greenhouse will tend to be pruned in the cane and spur method, covered earlier in this chapter.

The quality, taste and overall sweetness of grapes are also improved by thinning the fruit at least once during the early stages of the growing season, when the grapes are still small.

Harvesting

Grapes are ready for picking when they taste sweet and look 'heavy' hanging on the stalks. It is important to taste a variety of grapes to ensure that they are ready across the whole crop – however, being in the same atmosphere and in a relatively small space (in comparison to a vineyard), it is unusual for the crop not to be ready at the same time, if they are all from one variety.

As with a vineyard harvest, use snips to remove the grapes in whole bunches with a small amount of stalk attached. Take care reaching for higher-up bunches when at ground level; even when the crop is within reach, it can be precarious for both the picker and the vine if you find yourself stretching to snip a bunch which results in either you or the grapes – or both – falling and bruising unnecessarily! A decent stepladder and basket you can slip over your arm are often good tools to have at harvest time, so that you can place the fruit next to you after picking and not have to go up and down the ladder each time with small amounts of fruit.

Remember, grapes for eating will be dealt with differently to grapes destined for wine and it is best to eat or sell on your crop as soon as you can after harvesting, to ensure that they are enjoyed in top quality.

Sauvignon Blanc grapes being grown at Polgoon vineyard, Cornwall.

Greenhouse-grown Muscat producing delicious and delicate soft fruit.

CHAPTER 4

FRUIT

STRUCTURE OF THE GRAPE

It is important to understand what you will receive in the winery, as all aspects of the grape and stalk can impart flavour, some that are desirable and some less so. The stalk, for example, can contain some interesting *tannins* and impart phenolic character into wines. Like so many old wine-making techniques, making wines with some stalks has seen a resurgence, with growers claiming that the use of stalks in wine making can lead to enhanced finesse and character. When using the stalk, it is best to ensure that it is ripe, or the tannins will be potentially bitter, green and would not add pleasant flavours to the wines.

The majority of sparkling wine now produced in the UK is whole-bunched pressed, meaning that all of the fruit, including the stalk, is added to the press. The reason for this is to have less of the phenolic flavour from the skin, but also to retain more acidity. *Crushing and destemming* releases more potassium, which can remove acid from the juice and the finished wine, potentially rendering wine destined for sparkling to be lacking in the required levels of acidity for sparkling wine production. The stems and stalks are also known to remove some of the colour if one is whole-bunch pressing red grapes, which is relevant for the production of white sparkling using Pinot Noir or Pinot Meunier. The stalks also allow for greater run-off space in the press, meaning that the fruit inside the press does not become as 'caked' together as it often can do if one is pressing destemmed fruit.

Fantastic fruit ready for harvest at Astley Vineyard in Worcestershire.

OPPOSITE: Whole-bunch pressed Pinot Noir in a Coquard Press at Galleywood Vineyard in Essex.

Free-run juice coming off the press at Defined Wine Winery in Kent.

The grape is the perfect fruit from which to produce an alcoholic beverage, as it produces just the right levels of sugar, acidity and flavour compounds to make a balanced drink. No other fruit is packed with such a balance of parts to deliver this level of alcohol. The nearest fruit to the grape in this regard is the apple, which, although containing much flavour and character to produce a delicious drink in its own right, cannot deliver the required alcohol levels as those of the grape. With its perfect structure to hold sugar, acid and flavour together, it is worth understanding the component parts of the grape, to explore from where you can derive flavour to make the best possible wine.

Physically, the grape is made up of skin, *pulp* and seeds. Although the skin only accounts for a very small percentage of the grape, it has a significant impact on the finished wine. The skin contains tannin, aroma compounds and potassium, and produces all the colour. How long the juice is in contact with the skins and the temperature of the juice will decide the colour and the strength of aroma of the final wine.

As white wine is in contact with the skins for a short period of time, it should be considered how to elongate this so as to extract the maximum amount of aroma. This could be a cold *maceration* period prior to fermentation, or it could also be considered how to crush and destem to extract more phenolics into the juice. This is also true of red wine making and a cold maceration period is also known to increase varietal aroma.

When producing red wine, the temperature at which the fermentation occurs is also going to increase – or decrease – the amount of colour that can be extracted from the skins. It is worth noting that there is only so much colour that can be extracted from each varietal; for instance, Pinot Noir is not going to be able to produce the same depth of colour as Rondo, as the skins are much thinner.

Grape pulp contains all of the liquid and sugars that go into wine. These sugars are mainly fructose and glucose. As the grape ripens there is an equal balance between the two types of sugar, but as the grape

Foot-pressing red grapes – an ideal way to extract the colour throughout the fermentation.

reaches full maturity, fructose becomes the dominant sugar. During a standard fermentation, glucose will be fermented first and fructose next – this is because the yeast *Saccharomyces cerevisiae* prefers glucose, which can also be a cause for sluggish or stuck fermentations as the nutrients deplete with the glucose. What is left can be less nutrient and less glucose, which can cause the yeast to come into difficulty. However, all being well, the fermented *grape must* will result in alcohol production and carbon dioxide. The seeds are always present with a red wine fermentation, but not with white wine, as seeds are astringent and should be avoided where possible.

In cool-climate wine making, it is often the case that sugars are in high demand, whereas there can be an abundance of acidity. It is this balancing act that will ultimately decide the success of a wine and the best-suited production style. If low sugar but high acid, the best option is likely to be sparkling wine. If lower acid and higher sugar, the more obvious choice would be still wine production. If the wine maker works closely with the grape grower (or is the grape grower), there will be the opportunity to pick the grapes at a stage where both sugars and acid are in balance.

TIMING OF THE HARVEST

After a long growing season, grapes can start to come into ripeness from the end of August – at the earliest – all the way through to the start of November, depending on the variety and where in the country the fruit is growing. Varieties like Pinot Noir Precoce and Ortega are the first to be picked, with Seyval Blanc, Sauvignon Blanc and Pinot Noir being some of the last. As the fruit starts to become ripe, it is your responsibility as the grower to monitor the ripeness levels and have a plan in mind as to when you want to pick the fruit. Ultimately, the style of wine that you would like to produce should dictate when you pick.

Monitor the fruit using a refractometer to measure the sugar levels and a basic acidity testing kit to test acid levels. As the season starts to tail off and becomes cooler, sugar levels will increase at a much slower rate and may even seem to stall. However, you should notice that acidity levels continue to decrease at a steady rate and phenolic ripeness increases, so it is worth holding on before you pick, not only for increased sugar levels but riper fruit and a natural softening of the acids inside the fruit.

Timing is so important to the success of the harvest. This was late-harvested super-ripe fruit that became Pét-Nat.

Sparkling wine production is less reliant on perfectly ripe fruit than still wine making. In fact, some may argue that making good sparkling wine is easier to produce than good still wines. With time, acidity will drop, as will *tartrates*. The secondary fermentation process will also allow for there to be an extra flavour dimension to the wines and ultimately you do not require sparkling wines to be filtered, just careful *racking*. However, do be aware that any 'off' flavours will be magnified if not corrected as early as possible.

Fruit from Young Vines

To get fruit from a newly planted vine it will normally take three to four years from planting to achieve a crop. For the long-term benefit of the vine, all efforts should go into the growth and health of the vine as opposed to fruit production in the first few years, with a focus on removing competition for the vine to thrive, especially any unwanted growth from its trunk and any lateral growth. By not rushing the vine, you will enhance its longevity and its ability to produce more fruit year on year.

It is of course tempting to try to get fruit in the second year, especially if the vine has been growing well in year one; but remember that everything you do is about the long term and the vineyard's overall health over many decades, not just for one harvest.

Optimum Fruit

Simply put, if you would not eat the grapes yourself, you should not make wine out of them. The fruit should be clean with no disease, preferably with no wasp or bird damage. The fruit should be soft to the touch, ripe and have a balanced flavour. Ideally it should taste sweet, but of more importance is the balance of flavours. Grapes that are ready to pick will have brown or going-brown pips and the stalks that are holding the bunch onto the vine will be becoming thinner. Bunches of grapes will fall as the weight of the fruit becomes greater than the stalk can hold.

Birds and Insects

This timing of harvest is often tricky. As the fruit becomes riper, it will attract wasps and birds that will want to start eating the fruit – and with bird and insect damage comes diseased fruit. It is crucial to keep an eye on what is happening on site and to have a plan in place to stop the fruit being eaten. If you have a vineyard with lots of birds, you may consider netting to stop them eating the fruit, or other things to deter them like dummy kites and bangs, which can be an effective deterrent.

Insects are often trickier to deal with and for small vineyards a good solution can be attracting the insects to other sources of sugar. You can successfully use jams,

Wasps can take a large proportion of fruit in only a few weeks.

ciders, beers and other sugary items to draw wasps away from the fruit on the vine; an inexpensive method of safeguarding your crop.

YIELD

How much fruit to expect will depend on all of the factors involved with where you have sited your vineyard. Aim to produce two good bunches of fruit per shoot, as in a cool climate this ratio should ripen the fruit you have whilst not over- or under-doing the vine's potential.

Yield per acre will also be a direct consequence of your pruning techniques. If there are plenty of nodes on the vine (and if you escape late frosts and have a warm, sunny spring with ideal flowering conditions, followed by a mostly dry summer), there should be a decent crop. If you have left too many nodes on the vine and have a poor spring and summer, the crop will most likely be poorer in regard to weight and quality.

Nice healthy yield on the vine.

Always try to prune in a way that suits the vine and not on the prospect of a warm summer. Yields should be somewhere in the region of 3–5 tonnes per acre in good conditions, with poorer conditions more like 1–3 tonnes per acre. If you have a terrible summer – which will be about once a decade – then expect and be prepared for under a tonne per acre or even complete failure.

If you do have good fruit set from a nice spring, but the summer is not warm, consider green-harvesting your fruit. This early harvesting of some of the crop will direct sugars to the remaining fruit and will give you a higher-quality crop, even if less volume. However, this can only really be undertaken with experience of your vines – therefore you may need to trial this for a few years on a select few vines to find out if losing crop does result in higher-quality fruit.

When is a Vine Too Old?

Vines, as they age, produce fruit that is more complex to the taste and of a higher quality for making wine. Younger vines are often more fruitful, but lack the complexity of the fruit that is gained from older vines.

In theory, a vine never gets 'too old'. What will be witnessed, however, is that the more pruning wounds there are on a vine, the harder it will be for a vine to bring water through its trunk and so if these outlets become blocked then ultimately the vine will become less fruitful. As this happens, the vine can be retrained on new shoots that come from the base of the vine where there are no wounds. This creates a scenario where you have older roots and a younger trunk that should – if looked after – have all the vigour of a young vine, but with the mature roots of an old vine; a system of regeneration that means you should be able to work with that vine for many years.

In recent years there has been renewed interest in the *Guyot-Poussard* training system. This system encourages optimal sap flow within the vine, smaller pruning wounds, pruning ideally to take place on younger wood and when the sap is rising, and to understand that every cut on the vine will create dieback within the vine that will impede sap flow.

The lifespan of a vine comes down to stress on the plant. In a cool maritime climate like in the UK, vines are under a lot of stress as the weather is so variable, with weather systems that are up and down, meaning that the vine goes from hot, to cold, to wet. Added to this, producing fruit creates extra pressure that can lead to the vine having a hard existence, therefore every effort should be put in place so as not to overstress the vine and to make sure that it is supported with the correct amount and type of nutrients.

SUGARS AND ACIDS

Sparking Wines

The ideal sugars and acids to make different styles of wine greatly differ. One of the main reasons why cool-climate viticulture leads to very good sparkling wines is because the parameters are ideal for its production. It is not desirable to have high sugars; rather, it is desirable to have a level of sugar in the grape that, when the wine is put through secondary fermentation and the further increase in ABV, will not taste 'hot' or contain too much alcohol. Combined with the ability to *chaptalize* (the process of adding sugar) the must, the creation of sparkling wine in the UK is actually very favourable and the parameters can be quite forgiving.

This is also true for acidity. With high-acidity wines, there are a number of tools at the wine makers' disposal – including *de-acidification* and *malolactic fermentation* (MLF) – that can have an effect on the finished product. With finished wine, chemical de-acidification can legally reduce a wine's acidity by 2 grams per litre (g/l) TA. MLF plus the ageing process that will cause further de-acidification means that the resulting parameters for acidity can actually be quite significant.

White and Rosé Wines

To produce quality white wine, the fruit ideally needs to have higher sugars and lower acids than when producing sparkling wine. This means that your vineyard either needs to grow different grape varietals than sparkling varietals, or, as a grower, you need to keep the fruit on the vine longer so that it has the opportunity to ripen further and for sugars to rise and acids to drop.

Harvesting the fruit is a great day and the culmination of plenty of hard work in the vineyard.

Sparkling Wine Parameters

	Good Sparkling	Average	Poor
Sugars (potential ABV)	9.5–11%	7.5–9%	6.5–7.5%
Total acidity (TA)	8–11 TA	12–14 TA	14+

Pinot Noir is a great variety for sparkling wines as well as red and rosé. Some producers will even produce a white still wine from the variety.

White and Rosé Wine Parameters

	Ideal	Good	Average
Sugars (potential ABV)	11–12%+	9–11%	<9%
Total acidity (TA)	6–8 TA	8–10 TA	10+ TA

Red Wine

Red wine parameters are similar to white and rosé wines. The fruit needs to be allowed to become fully ripe and to develop all of its flavours on the vine. The sugars are the most important parameter here and the riper the fruit, the more desirable finished red wine. The fruit should be left on the vine for the longest possible period, so that it can rise in sugars and gain phenolic ripeness and complexity.

If wines do not have the desired level of sugar, it is possible to chaptalize to raise the sugars to bring them into the desired zone. However, this can lead to thin red wines and is a reason why red wine should only really be made during exceptional years in cool climates.

Acids should also be in the desired zone and if the juice or wine has to be manipulated, this can lead to wines that taste acidic and a little 'spiky'. For cool-climate viticulture it is often wise to put reds through MLF so that they are as soft as possible. In the UK, there will often be plenty of acidity to build the wine around and for MLF to combine really nicely with the wine as it ages. Oak ageing should also be considered, as this will soften the wine further. Old oak is often preferred to new oak, as cool-climate wines are mostly delicate and floral and too much oak character can overpower these subtle soft fruit characteristics.

Red Wine Parameters

	Ideal	Good	Average
Sugars (potential ABV)	12–15%	10–12%	<10%
Total Acidity (TA)	6–8 TA	8–10 TA	10+ TA

PHENOLIC RIPENESS

In many ways, it is easier to pick based on phenolic ripeness – physiological ripeness – than it is by sugars or acids alone. Phenolic ripeness is used to judge the ripeness of the grapes instead of relying only on analytical methods, such as testing sugar levels. Phenolic ripeness can be judged by how the pips look, how the fruit looks on the vine, how the stalk appears and how the leaves are faring. When phenolic ripeness

Bringing the fruit in at Astley Vineyard in Worcestershire.

is present, the pips will be brown, the fruit will be soft to touch and there will often be a layer of bloom on the grapes. The stalks that hold the fruit will start to wither and shrink, while the leaves on the vine will no longer be as green as they were during the height of summer. The fruit itself should taste in balance and delicious.

Phenolic ripeness is an interesting subject, as during the warmest summers for vines that are planted in a cool climate, these vines will struggle to reach phenolic ripeness, as the sugars will have risen and the acids will be dropping at too fast a rate outside of the desirable zone. As the climate gets warmer, however, it could lead to a vineyard having to be replanted with varieties that are more suited to the new weather conditions, so that phenolic ripeness and grape maturity in regard to sugars and acids can be reached at the right moment and not be too far out of kilter.

This is a challenge for all wine-producing parts of the world and it will be interesting to see how the UK reacts to this challenge. Will it continue to produce as much sparkling in the south of the country and buy yeasts that help to produce lower ABV wines, or will we see entire vineyard sites being converted to still wine production? Whatever happens, we know in the UK that there is a tremendous appetite for greater production of still wines, so we are in a great position to thrive.

CHAPTER 5

THE HARVEST

As the growing season draws to a close – usually between the months of September to November, depending on what varieties are planted – the decision arises of when to harvest. Harvest is one of the most exciting and joyous times in the vineyard cycle; a culmination of all the hard work and many hours spent tending the vines and getting the fruit safely in is one of the most rewarding experiences. Various low-cost equipment exists that will help with the decision of when best to pick. However, if you are making the judgment without any of these, the grapes themselves will offer a number of telltale signs.

Ripe, soft fruit.

OPPOSITE: **Bringing the fruit in even at a small vineyard can be a logistical challenge.**

SIGNS THAT THE FRUIT IS READY

The stalks that the grapes hang from will turn from green to brown and tend to get thinner when the fruit is ripe. The fruit will even begin to fall; in fact, whole bunches of grapes can often be harvested by hand without even the need for snips or secateurs – although this is not recommended – and this is why a decent pair of household scissors can often be of good-enough quality to harvest fruit successfully.

A second way of knowing that the fruit is ready to be harvested is by looking at the grape pips, which will also have changed colour from light green to brown. Lastly, tasting the fruit is a huge indicator. If it tastes sweet and pleasant, this usually means it is ready to be picked. Experience gained over the years will help you to really get to know the taste of a grape at its optimum moment for picking, but grapes destined for wines generally hold more sugar than table grapes and they are also higher in acidity. Remember, you need this acid as much as the sugar, so this should come through on tasting. The fruit should be soft to the bite, sweet and with a balanced taste.

Easy to use, cost-effective equipment is available for the run-up to harvest time, enabling growers to make an educated decision about when to harvest, but also about what style of wine to go on to make. Testing the sugar and acid levels of the fruit ultimately decides when it is best to harvest and a refractometer in the vineyard or *hydrometer* in the winery will test the sugar levels of the crop, while an acidity testing kit covers the acid content.

SUGARS

Knowing the level of sugars allows you to make an educated decision on the optimum time to pick. However, harvesting in a cooler climate can be challenging and it may be that you will have to pick at the final safe moment before cold snaps start to occur, as opposed to being able to wait for the sugars to reach ideal levels.

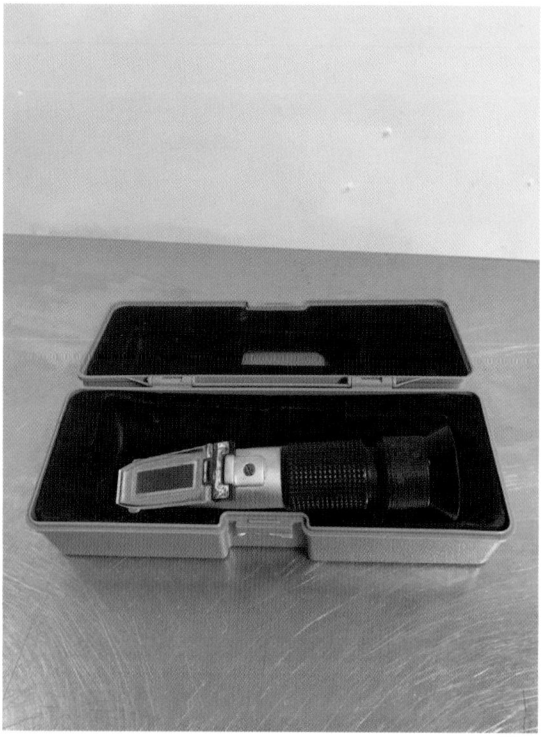

A refractometer is the best bit of kit as harvest approaches.

Hydrometer being used during harvest to measure density in the grape juice and sugars.

A crucial factor in the sugar levels of the fruit lies in whether you are producing still or sparkling wines. If sparkling, the ideal range of potential alcohol (sugar) falls between 9.5 per cent and 11.5 per cent. Above this, the wines may contain too much alcohol after the secondary fermentation for the desired style. If you are producing still wine, there's more freedom with sugar levels because there is no secondary fermentation and the styles of dry white and red wines can handle more alcoholic content in the finished wine.

If the fruit does not contain high sugars, the juice can still be chaptalized so that the sugars can be raised to a level that will produce palatable wine. The rules vary depending on in what country the crop is grown; those with cooler climates can raise sugar levels by up to 3 per cent potential alcohol in a standard year and 3.5 per cent potential alcohol in cooler years. Wine makers can find it disappointing having to raise sugars in this way, but the finished wine in these scenarios will nearly always benefit from having increased alcohol.

To work out sugar levels, the easiest way is to use either a hydrometer if you are in the winery, or a refractometer if you are in the vineyard.

Hydrometer

The hydrometer works by measuring the density of the grape juice versus the density of water; grape juice is denser than water and the buoyancy is mostly

Relationship between Oeschle, Potential Alcohol and Sugar

Oeschle	Potential Alcohol	Sugar g/l	Oeschle	Potential Alcohol	Sugar g/l	Oeschle	Potential Alcohol	Sugar g/l
44	5.1	87	67	8.7	148	89	12.2	207
45	5.3	90	68	8.9	151	90	12.4	209
46	5.5	92	69	9.1	154	91	12.5	212
47	5.6	95	70	9.2	156	92	12.7	215
48	5.8	98	71	9.4	159	93	12.8	217
49	5.9	100	72	9.5	162	94	13	220
50	6	103	73	9.7	164	95	13.1	223
51	6.2	106	74	9.8	167	96	13.3	225
52	6.4	108	75	10	170	97	13.4	228
53	6.6	111	76	10.2	172	98	13.6	231
54	6.7	114	77	10.3	173	99	13.8	233
55	6.9	116	78	10.5	178	100	14	236
56	7	119	79	10.6	180	101	14.1	239
57	7.2	122	80	10.8	183	102	14.2	241
58	7.3	124	81	10.9	186	103	14.4	244
59	7.5	127	82	11.1	188	104	14.5	247
60	7.7	130	83	11.3	191	105	14.7	249
61	7.8	132	84	11.4	193	106	14.9	252
62	8	135	85	11.6	196	107	15	255
63	8.1	138	86	11.7	199	108	15.2	257
64	8.3	140	87	11.9	201	109	15.3	260
65	8.4	143	88	12	204	110	15.5	263
66	8.6	146						

created by the presence of sugars. There are a number of ways of calculating the amount of sugar in the juice, including *Brix, Baume, specific gravity* (SG) or *Oeschle*. For the purposes of this book, we will be using SG or Oeschle as the methods of measuring sugars – types widely used in the UK. Included here is a table that shows the relationship between Oeschle, potential alcohol and sugar. In a cool climate, these readings are important to know early if the fruit is on its way to achieving high sugars, or if the fruit will need to be left on the vine as long as possible.

To get a true reflection of the potential alcohol in the fruit in the vineyard, it is best to extract juice from approximately 100 random grapes in the vineyard and homogenize the juice. This is easily done by squashing the grapes in a clean bag, then taking the juice from there. This juice should then be added to a trial jar. The hydrometer is then placed in the jar and the reading is taken.

The hydrometer can be used throughout the fermentation process, so that the depletion rate of fermentable sugars can be monitored, allowing the producer to know early if there are any potential issues with the juice.

Refractometer

For instant readings whilst on site in the vineyard, a refractometer is the best way to take a measurement. This pen-length piece of equipment gives an accurate indication of the sugars of the crop, if used across a number of samples. Ensure that the refractometer has been calibrated with water so that it gives a reading of zero before using it on juice. Once you have it calibrated and dried, simply squeeze a small amount of juice on the window of the refractometer and look through the sight glass. The refractometer works by taking a refractive measurement versus water, which reads at zero. It is important to take a number of measurements of the same crop and then get an average of the sugars from the number of samples that were taken.

MEASURING ACIDS AT HARVEST

Although sugar levels are often considered to be the most important parameter to wine making, careful

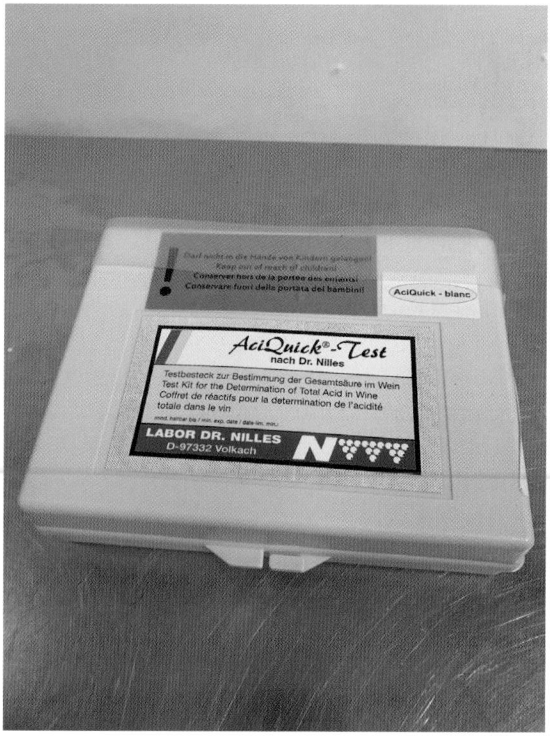

Fruit should be harvested based on acid as well as sugar; this testing kit is ideal for a fast reading.

consideration of the acids within the grapes is also vital, as already covered in this book. While the sugars are increasing in the grape, the acids are dropping. If the end of season weather is poor, it is often better to pick on the acid levels as opposed to the sugar levels, as sugars are relatively easy to rectify, whereas acid changes can have a more profound effect on the finished wine, which can be more difficult to resolve.

Chemical de-acidification is a particularly brutal process, leading to wines that can taste like they have been tampered with, whereas a biological de-acidification in the form of MLF or via blending is definitely preferred. MLF will offer complexity and there are a number of different types of bacteria available that can de-acidify and also raise the fruitiness of a finished wine (more on MLF in Chapter 6).

BALANCE

The key element in the sugar/acid relationship is balance. For most people, a good wine tastes 'balanced'. This is the relationship between sugar, acidity and astringency (in the form of tannin); three of the four taste areas of the tongue. The acidity forms the framework of the wine and is essential not to only sparkling wines, but also to wines that are worth ageing, for acid is required structurally so that a wine can develop.

Relatively low-cost acid-testing kits are widely available to measure the total acidity of the fruit. It is important to know the TA not just from a picking perspective, but also as the juice ferments into wine. The TA can be tested throughout the life cycle of the product. As the juice and subsequently the wine ages, the acidity will drop.

TA represents all of the acids in the grape, the most significant being tartaric, malic and citric. TA is often expressed in grams per litre and sometimes in a percentage of the weight to volume. A normal range could be as low as 5TA for early ripening Germanic varieties for example, through to 15TA for varietals suitable for sparkling wine making. Once levels reach above 15TA, there would be a definite case for chemical de-acidification.

PICKING GRAPES TO TEST LEVELS

How you pick grapes to test sugar and acid levels is of importance in the complete harvest process, as it is easy to choose the ripest fruit from a bunch when taking a reading and obtaining inaccurate results, which could result in picking too early. The fruit that is measured should be reflective of the *whole* vineyard, therefore take the time to select grapes – ideally without looking – from the top, middle and bottom of the fruiting zone.

Walk the rows and pick approximately 100 individual grapes at random, then take a reading from the hand-pressed juice. This process should start approximately three weeks before harvest and can be repeated right up to the harvest itself. If done every three days, you

A decent pair of snips are required for harvest.

will be obtaining an accurate overview of how the fruit is developing as harvest approaches, while also allowing you to organize pickers and logistics for the harvest in good time.

In summary, taking a sugar reading with a hydrometer/refractometer and performing acidity tests using a testing kit (and ultimately your own senses) are the best way to decide how and when you should be picking your crop.

HARVESTING OUTDOOR GRAPES – THE ESSENTIALS

Harvesting a vineyard of any size requires planning and preparation. Essentially you will need:

- pickers/volunteers
- snips
- picking crates
- vehicle to take the fruit to where the wine is being made.

Pickers

How fast the crop can be picked will depend on a number of factors, such as how the vine has been trellised and whether or not the vineyard has been leaf-stripped. If the vineyard is on a standard VSP system and the fruiting zone has been leaf-stripped, picking becomes a much quicker task. An effective picker will harvest around 250kg in an eight-hour day, but rates and speeds vary depending upon experience. It is hard work, so do ensure that you get support – do not try to harvest alone!

It is also meant to be a fun experience and a hugely rewarding thing to do, especially if the pickers are volunteers. Ensure that there are plenty of people, so that you are not putting any unnecessary pressure on pickers in an unrealistic timeframe.

Pickers will need snips/secateurs for the task. As the fruit becomes riper, it also becomes much easier to snip the stalk that connects the whole bunch to the vine. Ideally, try to keep the grapes entirely intact and to snip the least amount of stalk with the grapes as possible. Unless the wine maker is experimenting with extracting

Picking boxes need to be laid out on every row prior to harvest to help the pickers as much as possible.

Grape pickers ready to go bright and early at Blackdown Ridge Vineyard.

Dolav fruit picking bins are a great bit of kit for the small vineyard and the larger vineyard alike – when full, they hold around 300kg of picked fruit.

the flavour of stalk, this is not generally considered a desired flavour as it contains astringent green flavours and tannins.

Quality Control

Unless you have a sorting table where you make the wine, try to avoid picking any fruit that may have become damaged by pests such as wasps and birds, as well as removing any fruit that is past its prime. Unpleasant-looking fruit is not going to make good wine, so you have to be strict with quality control; if you wouldn't eat the fruit, you need to consider seriously whether you would want to make wine from it.

On a practical level, this means cutting out anything unpleasant from bunches, or simply not picking certain bunches at all. Training pickers and explaining exactly what is acceptable for harvest is crucial to the success of the finished wine; damaged or unhealthy-looking grapes, as well as under-ripe fruit, will have a detrimental effect on flavour if picked in large quantities. Or, if under-ripe fruit is picked, it should be kept separately in case you may need it to balance an over-ripe crop, instead of using chemical means.

When picking grape bunches, they should be placed into the picking trays and not just thrown in, as this can damage the fruit before the grapes get to the press and can lead to bruised flavours in the finished wine. This is especially important for wines that are destined for sparkling production.

Picking Trays

Picking trays need to be thoroughly cleaned prior to use and ideally should be sanitized the night before so that there will be no unwanted bacteria. A picking tray should be able to hold between 10 and 15kg of fruit. If it is too small, time will be lost carrying multiple small trays back and forth. However, if a tray is too large, pickers will become tired and not able to lift it, plus fruit at the bottom of the tray will become damaged by the weight of the fruit at the top.

It is also important that the trays are stackable, so that they can be loaded neatly into the vehicle without damaging the fruit within. Whether or not to opt for trays with vents depends on how long the fruit is going to remain in the crates. If for a short period only, there will be no detrimental effects on the fruit and the crates will not require vents. If, however, the crates are to be stacked for longer than twenty-four hours before pressing, it is better to use vented crates and allow for the loss of some juice, in order to prevent a wild fermentation. If this were to occur without any temperature control, it could, depending on the cleanliness of the fruit and the picking boxes, lead to the promotion of *volatile acidity* and potentially ruin the fruit. Pressing the fruit the day it is picked prevents these problems, but if the fruit does have to be left overnight ensure that it is stored in a covered, dry area and is as bug-free as possible.

Transportation to the Winery

If having to drive on major roads, it is best to hire an enclosed vehicle into which all the crates can be stacked. For the uninitiated, driving a trailer and fruit might be fine going to the winery, as it will not bounce around due to the weight of the crop, but coming back can lead to difficulties with loose crates in the back. After a long day in the vineyard and carrying (hopefully) hundreds of 10–15kg boxes, you don't want the final hassle of dealing with stray picking boxes!

If you are transporting your fruit to a neutral site, ensure that you have let the site know in good time when you plan on bringing it, as you want to get the fruit into the press as soon as possible after picking. Also ensure that you have a clear and agreed plan with the winery relating to your crop and its processing and, ultimately, its storage as wine.

Harvest Checklist

Following is a checklist for a 1–3 tonne vineyard:

- The more pickers, the merrier – lots of volunteers are there for a good time, not a long time! Be aware of this and see it as an opportunity to spread some goodwill and positive PR – and be thankful to them! Once someone does come and help harvest your vineyard, they may become a friend for life in the annual process. Aim to get as many people as possible to come along; advertise it as hard work, but also a social activity with the opportunity for a few glasses of wine afterwards (or during).

- Start as early in the day as possible, as harvest almost always takes longer than anticipated! Have a start and end time in mind, but be prepared to be flexible.
- Try to spread out pickers in allocated time slots, or get your volunteers to commit to a certain number of hours – there is nothing worse than everyone clearing off and leaving you to bring in the harvest on your own!
- Ensure plenty of clean trays/boxes.
- Ensure that there are plenty of clean snips available so that you don't need to rely on your workers (if volunteers) to bring their own.
- Supply a first-aid kit – someone will inevitably snip themselves during the day.
- Make sure that all of your picking boxes are clean, tidy and sanitized and that any stacking mechanism works.
- Designate tasks – for example, ask the stronger people to do the heavy lifting; send more experienced pickers down trickier rows.
- Ensure that there are plenty of breaks. For the inexperienced, harvesting is tough work and if the weather is hot ensure that plenty of water is available, or that people bring their own.
- Take lots of pictures – spread the word.
- Enjoy it!

In an ideal world, a flatbed on the back of a tractor will take the fruit to the winery – also useful for zipping around the vineyard.

Pickers working hard to fill the trailer at Astley Vineyard.

CHAPTER 6

WINE-MAKING TECHNIQUES

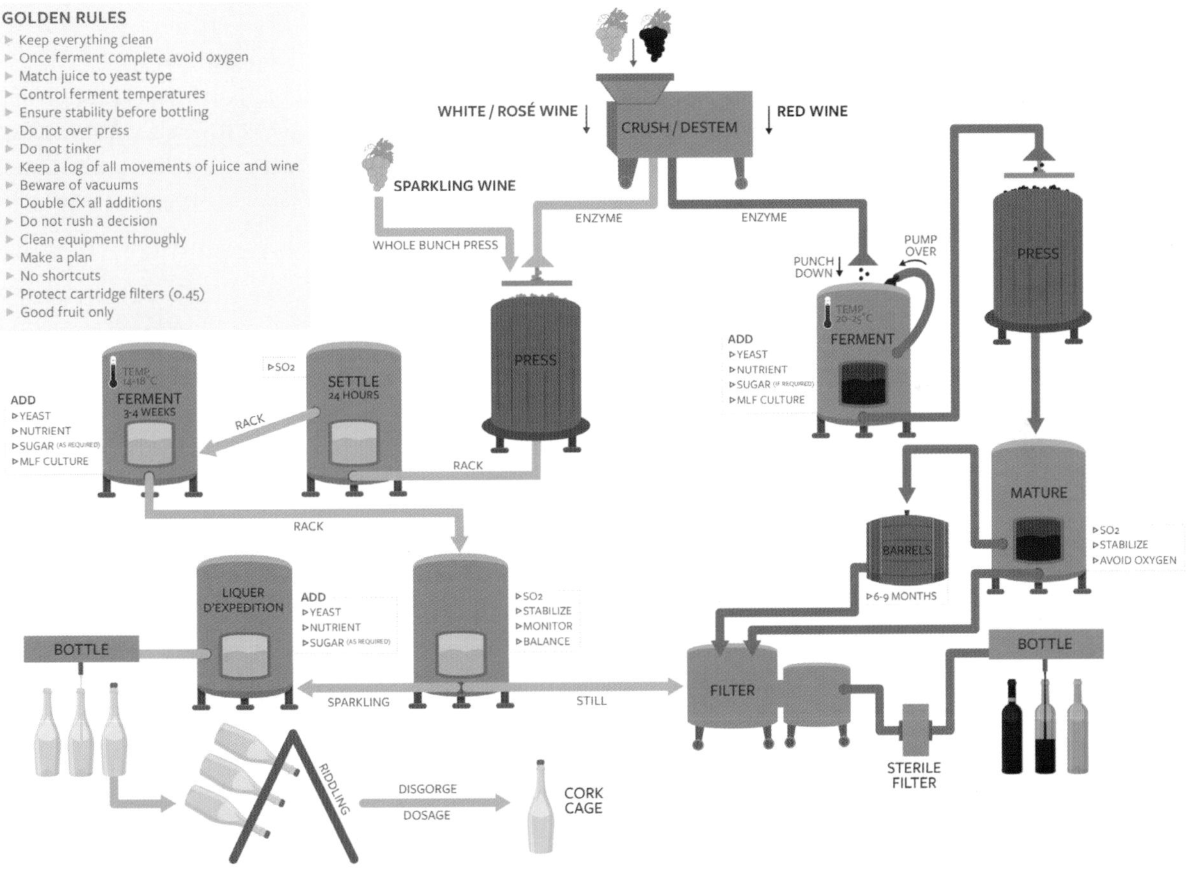

Diagram of the full wine-making process.

OPPOSITE: **Whole-bunch pressing in a basket press.**

BASIC EQUIPMENT

The fruit is harvested, now it's time to start making the wine. It is key to begin the process as soon as possible, as the grapes will deteriorate and be susceptible both to pests and acetic acid if left for too long.

If you are making wine in small quantities, even the most rudimentary equipment will see you through the process perfectly well. Every task can be carried out manually: from destemming the fruit, which can be done by hand; racking, which can be carried out with a syphon; pressing, which can be done either by hand or by foot; and a basic filtration, which can be achieved by careful racking and a pair of tights to take out any big solids.

To a certain level, this simplicity can translate to the winery, where one can be imaginative in the processes and the equipment to carry out each task, like using gravity to carry out all liquid movements, or *intermediate bulk containers* (IBC tanks) instead of stainless steel. With a little ingenuity, you can get most jobs done and it does not necessarily mean expensive equipment needing to be purchased. What is the most important requirement, however, is that you have knowledge of *why* you are doing what you are doing and how it will help you to produce good wine. The following list of equipment should cover all you need to produce wine efficiently.

Destemmers/Crushers

This does exactly what it says; it destems and can partially crush the fruit. There is often a setting on this equipment allowing you to change the crush setting so that it leads to a very light crush. When making white wines in particular, it needs to be on the lightest setting, as you want to be as gentle as possible with your fruit before it enters the press.

If producing red wine, the purpose of the machine is to destem and partially crush the fruit. The fruit then gets added whole (minus the stalk) to an open-topped fermentation vessel before adding in the yeast to the partially crushed grape. If stalks remain, they can be high in tannins and therefore can give green, astringent flavour to the finished wine.

Pumps

There are a large number of different pumps available to buy and each one comes with very different price tags. A small winery will often not need a pump, although they can be extremely helpful to get you out of a spot of bother if you need to move something quickly.

Remember, small-scale wine making does not need a pump and it can be carried out by lifting and carrying and syphoning with tubes. However, once it is no longer practicable to lift up the liquid in its container, it is time to use a pump.

If you are moving solids – must and grapes in the red wine – then you need to consider if you can carry out the process with the physical handling of buckets, or if you want to invest in an expensive, but excellent, peristaltic pump that is designed to handle solids. A regular pump would struggle to handle this. If you are buying a pump, ensure that you get the best possible advice from a specialist supplier and explain what

A small diaphragm pump is ideal in a small winery.

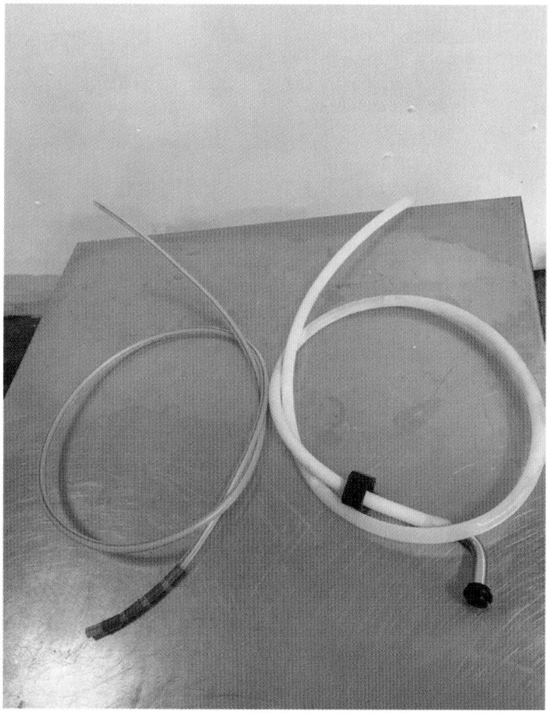

Siphons and small hoses can be very useful for moving small quantities of wine or juice.

processes you are expecting your pump to do. Here are some requirements and features of a wine pump to look out for:

- gentle process
- speed control
- low oxygen pick-up
- forwards and backwards movement of liquids is advantageous
- ability to move solids, as there will always be some in your wine
- easy to clean
- easily movable – most pumps can be put on wheels so that they can be moved around the winery if necessary
- budget

Presses

If you are making wine on a very small scale, the grape can be hand-pressed or foot-pressed and you don't need to buy a press at all. However, for the moderately sized producer (100kg plus), the entry-level press is going to be a hydropress or a hydraulic press.

Summary of Common Pump Types for a Small Winery

Pump	Diaphragm	Centrifugal	Impeller	Peristaltic
Pros	• cheap, easy to use • works off compressed air, so often only single-phase electricity is required • gentle • can run it dry with no damage to the pump • small and lightweight	• easy to obtain • cheap to buy • easy to use • high flow rate	• tolerant of sediment • easy to use	• does everything you want from a pump – gentle, speed control, low oxygen pick-up
Cons	• one direction only	• rough process on wine and liquids • limited speed control	• possible for parts to break off and enter into the liquid	• big • expensive

Peristaltic pump – a fantastic item for moving wine, juice and solids.

A hydropress is excellent for whole-bunch pressing of grapes.

Hydropress The hydropress works by inflating an internal bag with water, which expands and forces the grapes to be pressed between the bag and the inside mesh of the press basket. These types of presses are very easy to use and with a bit of practice can be set to give quite a soft press. Depending on the model of hydropress, you can also use compressed air, which often allows for more pressure into the bag and more control over the pressings. However, check if it is safe to do so; you certainly do not want a bag to explode with too much pressure in it!

Hydraulic press The hydraulic press often looks similar to the hydropress. However, this type of press does not expand with an internal bag, but instead screws down hydraulically. This can be done either manually or with a jack. These presses are very effective and tend to be widely available, as they are used extensively in the cider world.

Pneumatic press If you are pressing larger quantities, you may choose to buy a pneumatic press. These presses often come with a host of features and press-cycle programs that can provide plenty of control, including press, crumble and spin, and ultimately they will extract more juice than the above options are able. This does not necessarily mean

Whole-bunch pressing in a pneumatic grape press at Defined Wine in Kent.

that they are any better, however, as with greater extraction, much of what is being extracted at the end of the process can be of lesser quality compared with the juice extracted at the start. Nevertheless, the pneumatic press is undoubtedly more convenient if you are dealing with larger quantities of fruit.

Vessels

You need to put your juice in something once pressed. This should be of a similar size in litres to the amount you are pressing; you don't want any head space for oxygen as this will lead to a higher likelihood of failure for your wine. Vessels could be plastic, stainless steel, fibreglass, glass, concrete or oak; the most important element is that it is clean. If you use dirty vessels, wines will suffer and the end product will not be as good as it could be.

In an ideal world, you want to be able to have complete control of the fermentation temperatures and therefore some form of thermostat system is a welcome addition to the tanks. For the wine maker on a budget or with a small volume of wine, this could be access to a cold area or space if you are dealing with demijohns.

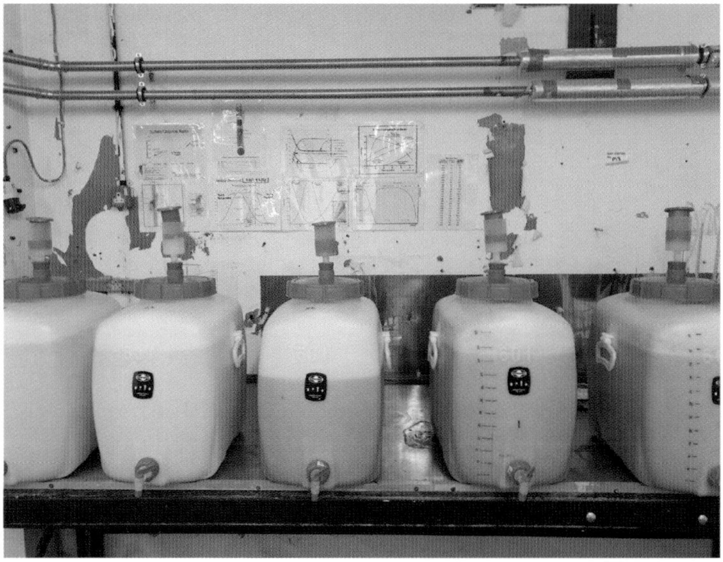

Small vessels, easy to clean and ideal for small-batch fermentations.

Fixed-capacity large stainless-steel tanks, some with temperature control, some without, the ideal vessel to retain varietal character.

If you are making red wine, your vessel needs to be open so that you can *punch down* the grape skins, or *pump over* the juice on top of the skins. The consideration thereafter comes with how to move the fermented grapes into the press, post-fermentation. Depending on the size of the operation, this can be achieved with buckets. However, once this is no longer practicable (in other words, your yield has grown), you either need a tank that has a manway door or a peristaltic/must pump.

If using a tank with a manway door, the tank can be lifted over the press and the racking valve can be opened into the press. Once the juice/wine is drained, the manway door can then be opened, allowing the grapes into the press. If using a peristaltic/must pump, it is designed to move solids (including grapes) and therefore is the ideal – and safer – option.

Your vessel should have the following attributes:

- ability to put an airlock in place
- easy to clean
- ideally a sample valve (non-essential, but useful)
- racking valve (non-essential, but useful).

Oak barrels – a fantastic tool in the wine-maker's arsenal; very hard to clean, but the positive impact on flavour is worth the challenges.

Fixed- and Variable-Capacity Tanks

Variable-capacity tanks If you are going to invest in stainless-steel tanks, a good option is to go for variable-capacity (VC) tanks. These vessels come with a blow-up lid, which means that they do not have to be completely full so as to avoid oxidation. Post-fermentation, the lids can be pumped up to a particular point on the tank and therefore the wine should be oxygen-free and in the best possible condition. It also means that if you are using red grapes in your production, the wines can be fermented in these vessels as you can punch down easily.

There are a couple of drawbacks to these tanks. One is that the floating lid has a tendency to deflate, so it is always a good idea to check the lid on a weekly basis to ensure that it is pumped up. The tanks can also be a bit trickier to clean and the floating lid can become grimy with grape juice, wine, dead insects and so on – so a little extra care is needed to ensure good sanitization and that nothing is clinging to this area of the tank.

Fixed-capacity tanks Fixed-capacity (FC) tanks, if to be used to capacity, are a great option in a winery as you know that the liquid inside the tank cannot become oxidized. If your tank is not full of juice, it is a good idea to invest in a carbon dioxide (CO_2) or nitrogen (N) canister to ensure that any remaining

Fixed-capacity temperature-controlled tanks, ideal for white wine fermentation.

space in the tank is purged with these gasses, as opposed to oxygen. This will ensure that the wine remains as fresh as possible.

Fixed-capacity tanks are more uniform in design and tend to look smarter in a winery, so if your facility is going to also be a form of visitor attraction, they set the right image for the consumer.

Barrels

If you are producing enough wine, the barrel is a great place to store it, not least because the barrel implants fantastic flavours to not only red wine, but also white wines and base wines destined for sparkling. If new, a barrel will impart an array of flavour depending on how it has been produced through the oak and the cooperage; this can swing from fresh and fruity through to rich and spicy. Careful consideration therefore must be given to the type of barrel used.

In cool-climate wine making, brand-new barrels need to be handled with care, as they can impart too much flavour for the delicate wine to handle. It is therefore of benefit to seek one-, two- or even three-year-old barrels that can still impart flavour. Renovated barrels can be a great tool also. The barrel also micro-oxidizes and in the process helps to stabilize colour and allows the wines to develop and soften.[7]

Barrel-aged wine can be used for blending with other wines to develop complexity within a product. Many of the UK's most successful sparkling wines will have seen some barrel ageing; this is often in the region of 5–10 per cent of the total wine.

Fermentation Locks

Ensure that whatever vessel you chose is equipped with a fermentation lock and bubbler – during fermentation, the bubbler will allow you to know when the juice, as it turns into wine, has stopped fermenting. It will also provide a useful indication of whether the wines are going through a malolactic fermentation. Once all bubbling has stopped, the fermentation has completely finished and the wine needs stabilizing and racking.

Using oak is not always about oak flavours, but micro-oxidation – old oak is a great vehicle for fermentation or storage.

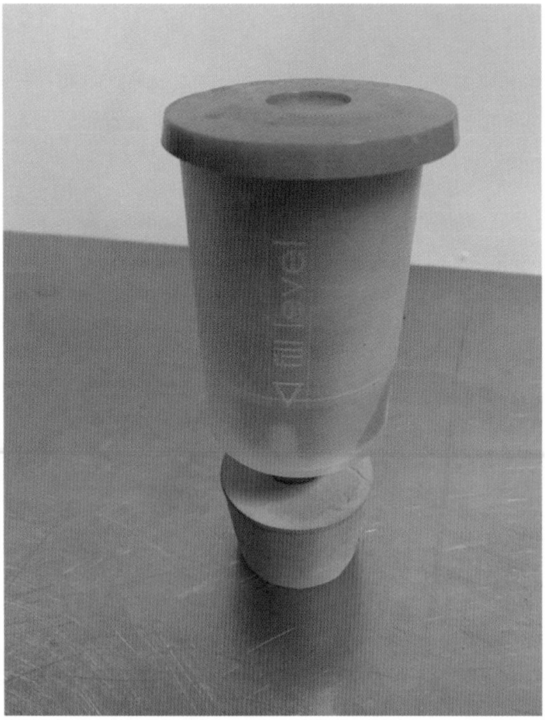

A bubbler and fermentation lock is a great indicator of when the fermentation has ended.

Siphons

Small-scale wine making will always require the ability to rack the wines off and – as already mentioned – if you are producing small quantities, it may not be practical to use a pump and therefore actually siphoning by using gravity, simply by lifting a demijohn, may be a better option. Siphons can be a long tube, or they can be solid instruments that are dipped in the liquid and when you put your thumb over the top of the tube it will hold the liquid inside it. This is commonly known as a 'wine thief' and is really handy if dealing with barrels or demijohns, as the wine can be extracted without disturbing the liquid inside.

Thermometers

Thermometers are used for a whole range of tasks in the winery. You need to know the fermentation temperatures of your juice; too hot, for example, and aromas will be lost. Taking temperatures will also give a good indication of when the fermentation is coming to an end, as the process starts to cool; combined with a hydrometer, this will provide the best indication. When starting the fermentation process with commercial yeast, a thermometer is also vital to ensure that you have the recommended temperature.

Hydrometers

You will need a hydrometer so that you can measure the journey from juice to wine, as refractometers do not work effectively for this task. A range of hydrometers will measure the liquid throughout the fermentation.

Acid-Testing Kits/pH

A basic kit will consist of phenolphthalein and sodium hydroxide (NaOH) at 0.1N. The sodium hydroxide is titrated against a known quantity of juice or wine with phenolphthalein. When the acid is neutralized in the wine or juice during the titration, it gives a reading that shows how much titratable acidity is in the liquid by turning a different colour. These kits are readily available through any good supplier of wine-making

Hydrometer measuring Pinot Noir juice from Carlton Towers Vineyard in Yorkshire.

equipment. Remember, you are required to know the acidity of your juice for picking purposes but also for wine making, so that you can make the correct decisions during production.

Scales

You will need a decent set of scales for all winery tasks so that you can measure the correct quantities of products including yeast, nutrient, MLF culture, sugar or potassium bicarbonate. Investing in two sets of scales can be a good idea. One can be a basic set of kitchen scales for general winery use and the other a very precise set of scales for measuring very small quantities of product like MLF bacteria.

Whisks/Spoons

A whisk/spoon is a must for a whole host of mixing tasks. An essential piece of winery kit!

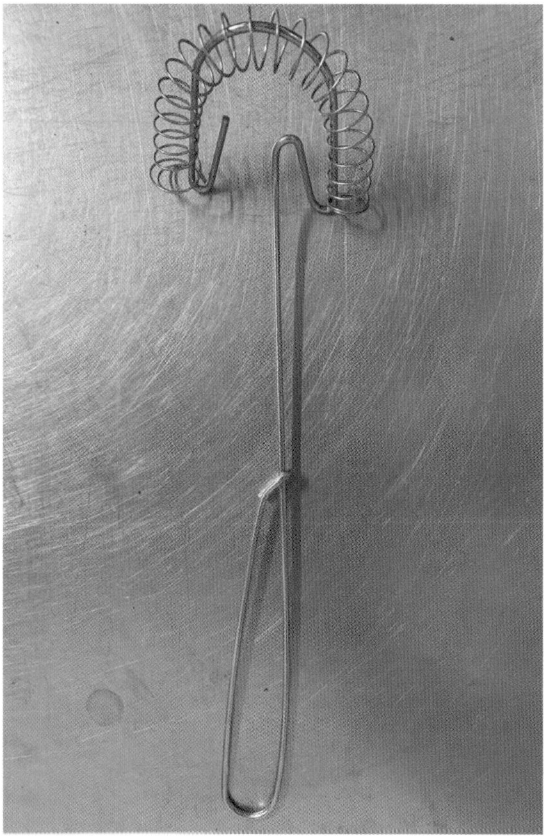

A small whisk is handy in any size of winery.

CLEANING AND STERILITY

Without doubt, for most wine makers, the words 'cleaning' and '*sterility*' are the terms that are the most troubling in the wine-making process. Sterility – or the lack of it – can be the difference between a good wine or a failed wine. The problem is often not the process of cleaning itself, but the kit and equipment used to do the cleaning.

Following an entire clean of the winery or your production space, every piece of equipment should be sanitized and anything that the wine comes in contact with should be sterile. A lack of cleanliness does not promote positive flavours – ever.

Cleaning and sanitizing can be achieved in a cost-effective manner and the most important aspect is promoting a culture of cleanliness in the winery. Being an expressive and artistic wine maker is great, but this must be combined with a commitment to cleanliness.

There can be physical reasons why a winery is not as easy to clean as it could be; for instance, the winery may be in an old barn with a floor that makes the draining of liquids difficult. Or the production area might be so full of wine tanks that space is tight and getting between the tanks is tricky. Whatever the reasons, these are also excuses and should never be accepted as a reason not to clean.

How do you approach cleaning wineries in difficult to reach spaces? First, you will need the correct PPE for the task. In the winery, this means: goggles to protect your eyes; gloves to protect any exposed skin; wellington boots (to be worn in the winery only); and ideally some form of coverall for the task. You certainly do not want to be exposing non-work wear to the task and you will need to have all skin safely covered up before using any equipment. You will also require a mop, bucket, brush and power-washer as the minimum kit in the winery.

It is advisable to keep a log that records when and where you have cleaned. This can then be used if your winery is going through any form of audit and, importantly, a broken-glass record sheet will be created, which is essential to the safety and cleanliness of the production space.

All forms of documentation, especially if going from no records to keeping records, can feel like a costly waste of time and resources; however, it can be invaluable proof that your business is doing everything it can to be as professional as possible. That, in turn, will increase the confidence in others visiting your business and raise the pride of those working there. Crucially, keeping a log of the cleaning process is also absolutely necessary if your business plans to sell to any of the UK supermarkets.

Cleaning

It is important to know what chemicals are available to use and when to use them, so that everything in the winery is as clean and sanitized as possible. Cleaning is arguably best carried out with caustic soda. Great care and attention should be taken when using this product, as caustic is an extremely strong alkaline that will cause very nasty burns if in contact with any part of the body. It is best used to clean stainless steel, but can also be used on floors. Always read the safety labels when using this product. Caustic is most effective when it has been warmed. It can be used effectively in any cleaning in place cycle (CIP) and will remove any stubborn debris.

Whatever item has been cleaned with caustic should then be rinsed thoroughly. It is best practice to check with pH strips to ensure that any residue has left the surface; pH strips measure potential hydrogen, with pH1 indicating extreme acid and pH14 extreme alkaline, whereas water is pH7, therefore neutral. Rinsing cannot be overlooked before you move on to the next stage – such as the addition of *peracetic acid* (PAA) – as there is a strong risk that your alkaline (caustic) combined with your acid (PAA) will cause a base (therefore neutralize the peracetic), meaning that you have been unable to sterilize successfully.

Sanitation

It can take some time to understand sanitation and to find an approach that will work every time, but it is important to do so. First on the list of sanitation products should be PAA. This product, once at the right solution, will sanitize anything. It is recommended to buy a testing kit to ensure that your PAA is at the correct dosage to achieve full sterility. Because PAA oxidizes, it will lose some of its strength over time, therefore if you were using a PAA solution across several days it might no longer have the strength to provide adequate sterility. It is best to mix a fresh solution every time.

To really get some peace of mind, combine PAA with an *adenosine triphosphate* (ATP) reading machine. ATP is an *enzyme* contained in all living things and by using the machine it is possible to ensure that there is nothing alive in the system such as yeast or bacteria.

If you are bottling, make sure that everything the wine comes into contact with has been cleaned with PAA; it is a contact-based sterilizer and therefore provides instant sterility.

In summary, the steps to sterility are:

1. Rinse with cold or, ideally, hot water and with a powerful jet wash if possible.
2. Use caustic soda (2 per cent solution) or a powerful organic version – check the strength of the caustic that you are using and follow instructions for use.

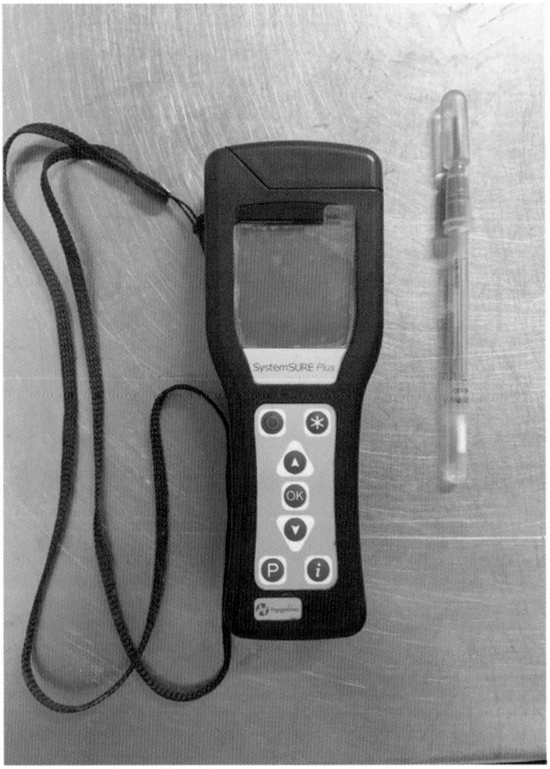

An ATP testing kit gives a great indication of whether your equipment is sterile.

3. Rinse the caustic with water and check with pH strips that no caustic remains.
4. Using a 2 per cent PAA flush will ensure that nothing can be living in your tank. If you have mixed the PAA and got it to all parts, it will work unless there has been an error in your process.
5. It is not obligatory to rinse PAA as it oxidizes so that the chemical is no longer active – it is down to personal preference as to whether you rinse it off or not. If you are rinsing, your rinse water needs to be sterile also.
6. Take a pH reading using pH strips. If it reads pH7 on the strip, you know that you are good to go; pH strips are so inexpensive that it is recommended always having them in the winery.
7. Take an ATP reading. Although an ATP reader is quite a sophisticated device to own, if you want peace of mind that your surfaces are entirely sterile, it is a worthwhile piece of equipment to have in the winery.

Whole-bunch pressing in a basket press – the yield will be around a barrel of juice (225l).

WINE-MAKING PROCESSES – WHITE WINE

There are many different, wonderful wine-making techniques and no two wine makers will do things exactly the same. Here we are focusing on the most straightforward methods – which often means the most effective. Using white wine as the model, the following techniques and processes will also apply across making rosé and red wines (sparkling wine will follow in Chapter 8).

The grapes are now picked and in the winery; your options are either to destem or whole-bunch press. The easiest route – especially if you have limited equipment available – is to whole-bunch press. Whilst it is true that there are tannins in stalks, by pressing gently these flavours should not end up in the finished wine. In fact, there can be benefits to keeping the stalks, such as easier run-off of juice, as the grapes are less caked in the grape press.

Add the fruit to whatever press you are using. If you are hand- or foot-pressing or using a hydropress, it is actually quite difficult to over-press. However, if using a hydraulic or pneumatic press, make sure that you do not exceed 2bar of pressure, or it is likely you will be over-pressing the grapes.

Press Fractions

Press fractions for white wine and sparkling base wine are crucial to the success of the finished wine. A lot of this will be learnt through experience, but, as a rule of thumb, once you exceed 1bar of pressure on your chosen machine, you should now be tasting the juice carefully in every press increment. The first hint of astringency and bitterness is the sign that you are over-extracting your juice and it is time to stop pressing.

It is also a good idea – especially if using a hydropress – to release the pressure and take a look at the grapes, allowing you to assess visually how much juice is left in them. If they are still visibly soft and wet to touch, there is still some juice left to be extracted from the grape. In fact, opening the press and releasing the pressure is similar to the process of using the celebrated Coquard Press, for whilst using these machines, it is part of the procedure to open the press and turn over the grapes. This approach to juice pressing can be replicated with a hydropress or hydraulic press, but instead of using a fork you will require a tool to prise the grape skins away from the press walls. Once done, you start the pressing process again.

Try to replicate a similar press cycle as given in the table. Even if using basic pressing kit, you can aim for these readings. The figures give an indication of the low pressures and the time that is required to extract the best juice.

Typical Grape-Pressing Cycle

	Cuvée	Cuvée	Cuvée	Taille	Taille	Taille
Pressure (bar)	Press 1 (seconds)	Press 2 (seconds)	Press 3 (seconds)	Press 4 (seconds)	Press 5 (seconds)	Press 6 (seconds)
0.2	540	420	360			
0.4	480	300	300	300	240	
0.6	300	360	360	300	240	240
0.8	360	420	360	300	300	240
1.0	420	360	360	300	300	300
1.2	300	300	300	300	360	360
1.4				300	300	360
1.6					300	300
Rotations	2	2	3	3	4	4

The principles of pressing gently can be applied to whatever press you are using.

In terms of extraction rates, try to achieve the following. For sparkling base wine you will be looking at 51 per cent of the weight of the fruit, so if your fruit weighs 100kg, you should be trying to extract 51l of juice. If you are pressing for still wines, these figures should be nearer 60–70 per cent extraction, so 60–70l respectively. Keep tasting the juice and once you taste astringent flavours it is better to separate that juice and decide at a later stage what to do with it.

Sulphur Dioxide

Sulphur dioxide (SO_2) is both anti-bacterial and anti-oxidative, and will prevent wild fermentations and spoilage from occurring in the short term, as well as preventing excessive browning of the juice.

The first time you add SO_2 is either during the pressing process or just after, once all of the juice has been extracted. Make sure that you know the quantity of juice you are working with before you add SO_2, so as to prevent using too much or too little. How much SO_2 to use is based on the following equation:

- 1g SO_2 = 10ppm (SO_2) @ 1hl

The juice should be at 40ppm, therefore if you have 100l or 1hl, the equation looks like this:

- 1g = 10ppm @1hl
- 4g = 40ppm @1hl

The type of SO_2 most used in wine making is potassium metabisulfite (PMS). This is approximately 50 per cent strength of SO_2, so the final figure needs to be multiplied by two, as follows:

- 4g = 40ppm @1hl
- multiplied by two if PMS = 8g (PMS) = 40ppm @1hl

When handling SO_2 always check your additions, as too much SO_2 in the wine can be dangerous for the consumer. Sulphur dioxide exists as free, bound and total. Free SO_2 is the element that protects the juice and wine, whereas bound is no longer a preservative, as SO_2 diminishes over time due to oxidation – becoming bound in the liquid. Therefore to ensure that your wine is safe from spoilage, it should always be in the region of 40ppm free SO_2. (More detail to follow in Chapter 7.)

SO_2 is a great tool for anti-oxidation and anti-microbial wine making. Always check the strength of the SO_2 in the packet or tub that you are using.

Enzyme

Enzymes are used in the wine-making process to speed up reactions that would otherwise happen more slowly, or not happen at all. The use of enzymes will generally result in a higher yield (there are other types of enzyme that are used to gain aroma or aid maceration if you are planning on producing a red wine, but the focus here is on white wine). The type of enzyme that you require at this stage is a pectinase enzyme to help extraction and clarification of the juice prior to fermentation. This will result in a cleaner juice that will lead ultimately to improved wines.

Additions

There may be times – especially for wines made in cool climates – that it will be necessary to make other additions aside of SO_2 and enzyme. Sugars, MLF bacteria, *fining* agents and yeasts are all options that can aid and enhance the wine during its production. Always know what you are using your additions for, read the instructions and always double-check your figures. If the quantities look like they are excessive or not enough, then they probably are!

First Rack

Once SO_2 has been added, the juice can sit for twenty-four to thirty-six hours in order to prevent solids within the clean juice being fermented. This is known as settling and takes places because solids can lead to unpleasant, green flavours in the finished wines.

Once racking commences, try not to disturb any of those solids (gross lees) at the bottom of your vessel – although if you do pick up a few lees, it isn't a huge issue as some solids will actually aid the fermentation. Racking the wines literally means moving wine from one vessel to another and it is done to prevent the juice sitting on gross lees for too long a period.

Clean juice being racked.

Once the clean juice is racked, now is the time to check the sugars and acids and make your final call as to what additions you may wish to make. Making additions after the first rack is the recommended time, as once the fermentation begins, if you add sugar (chaptalize) or potassium bicarbonate (de-acidify) at this stage it will lead to the juice becoming very excited and can force quite a violent reaction that will result in a lot of mess and wasted liquid. Rest assured, for the new wine maker these eruptions are a rite of passage to experience, but it is still advisable to make additions at the first racking.

Chaptalization

In the UK, it is legal to chaptalize the juice and raise the potential alcohol by up to 3 per cent ABV and – in very poor years – this can be raised by 3.5 per cent ABV if given approval, with maximums being placed on the style of wine that is being produced – 11.5 per cent for white and rosé wines and 12 per cent for red wines.

(If producing sparkling wine, you should be aiming for 10–10.5 per cent ABV for the initial fermentation, as there will be a further 0.8–1.2 per cent rise at the secondary fermentation stage – *see* Chapter 8.)

Ultimately, experience will guide you as to how much to raise the potential alcohol in your wines. To raise the potential alcohol by 1 per cent ABV, wine makers work off the addition of 17g/l of sugar. Therefore, if you are raising a juice by 3 per cent ABV, you will need 51g/l, which leads to a significant addition of sugar.

De-acidification

Like adding sugar, there are rules on how much you can de-acidify wines. Only consider chemical de-acidification if the wines are over 12g/l of total acidity. It is often better to allow time or MLF to carry out the de-acidification.

If you are chemically de-acidifying, the best product to use is potassium bicarbonate, as it is a more gentle addition than potassium carbonate. An addition of 1g/l will de-acidify the juice by approximately 1g/l. This process – if your juice is under 3.00pH – will also increase the pH level, making more favourable conditions for MLF. Combined with a long ageing period, it is generally possible to get the wines in a pleasant zone for drinking, that is, the correct balance between the acid and sugar.

If it is not possible or desirable to get the wines under 12g/l, you can consider blending the wine with something of a lower total acidity, or allow the wines to age for a considerable period of time. English wine really does benefit from ageing; often English wines are not given the time needed to be at their best.

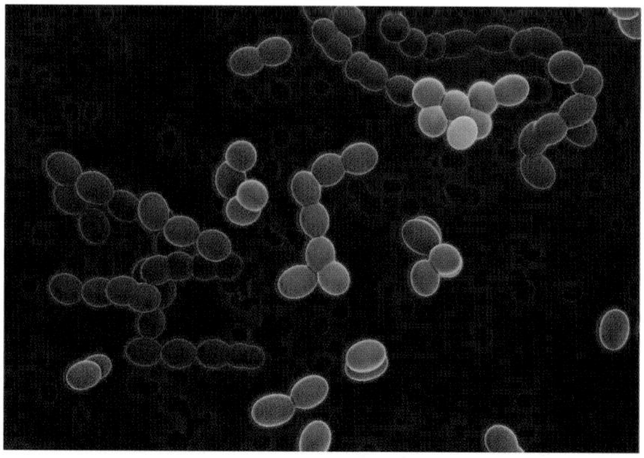

***Oenococcus oeni* bacteria responsible for MLF under the microscope.**

Fining

To aid the clarification stage of the juice, the fining stage can be done now. For cooler-climate environments, carrying out a bentonite fining using the minimum quantities should make the juice protein-stable. Protein *stability* will mean that no protein can appear in the bottle – which is something you definitely do not want to occur, as it appears in the bottle as a swirling white cloud that looks unpleasant to consume. By using the minimum quantities of bentonite, you won't be damaging the juice in any way. Always follow the guidance from the manufacturer of the bentonite.

Fining can also give a greater yield on pressed juice for the fermentation and importantly you are not making chemical changes to the wine when it is almost ready to be bottled, which can have quite a big impact and take the wine a number of months to fully recover from the changes. It is always recommended to get your wine analysed prior to bottling and one of the key parameters is protein stability. If your wines are not protein-stable, it will be necessary to conduct full fining trials to ensure that you are always using the minimal quantity of bentonite, as fining agents have been known to strip some flavour and aroma. (More detail to follow in Chapter 7.)

Bentonite for fining wine.

Yeast

Your juice should now be where you want it in terms of its sugar and acids levels, plus an addition of bentonite, racked and clear of large particles. The choice is now whether to allow nature to take its course and have a 'wild' fermentation, or whether to add a commercial yeast. When first starting out as a wine maker, it would be wiser to buy a commercial yeast to match your juice to ensure that you have less likelihood of problems.

Carry out your research with yeast and make a wine that suits the juice. Do not try to turn your juice into something that it is clearly not suited to being, or else while you may end up with something that is good, it perhaps could have been better. If you have low-sugar/high-acid juice, for example, use a yeast that marries what you are trying to achieve; do not aim for a high-alcohol wine, as it will be out of balance.

When handling yeast, always follow the manufacturers' guidelines, as some protocols will be different. Most yeasts will follow something similar to what is outlined below:

- Rehydration of the yeast using water is crucial to its success. Do not use grape juice to rehydrate yeast as the conditions will be too harsh for it. The yeast needs to wake up before confronting it with tough conditions.
- Monitor the temperature of the yeast and ensure that the start temperature is in line with what is stated on the packet. Most yeasts like 37–40°C.
- If you have unclean fruit, increase the quantity of yeast used – this could be raising the dose to 30g/hl instead of 20g/hl. You could even look into using a more powerful yeast strain.
- Add the yeast as soon as possible to the racked juice. It can be a good idea to make up the yeast culture and put it into the receiving tank, so that the juice can be brought into the tank with the

yeast already present and therefore be thoroughly mixed.

- There are other products to enhance the yeast at this stage and to ensure that you have a clean fermentation. These are products like yeast protectors, which can be especially useful to use in cool-climate wine making if your juice is very clear and has low solids.

If you follow the above and if your juice is not under 10°C, fermentation will begin. Remember that nutrition additions go hand in hand with yeast (*see* section on nutrients below).

Small-batch wine making is as much about using your senses as it is understanding the fermentation process. For example, after the yeast has been added, for a short period of time nothing seems to happen – this is known as the 'lag phase'. Once fermentation does start, you may see a visible 'current' forming as the juice is fermenting, or sightings of prickles on the juice, which indicates the growth phase.

If your juice is fermenting in a fixed-capacity tank containing a bubbler, you will witness the bubbler bubbling. This can be dramatic (during the growth phase), or quite steady and slowing down (during the growth into stationary phase). It is also obvious when the juice is becoming wine, as it goes from clear to opaque and cloudy. When the juice stops fermenting, the wine starts to clear. This is the 'death' phase, when the yeast has carried out its function and there is no longer any sugar to ferment.

In addition to visual tells, one of the most obvious ways of knowing if things are fermenting well is CO_2.

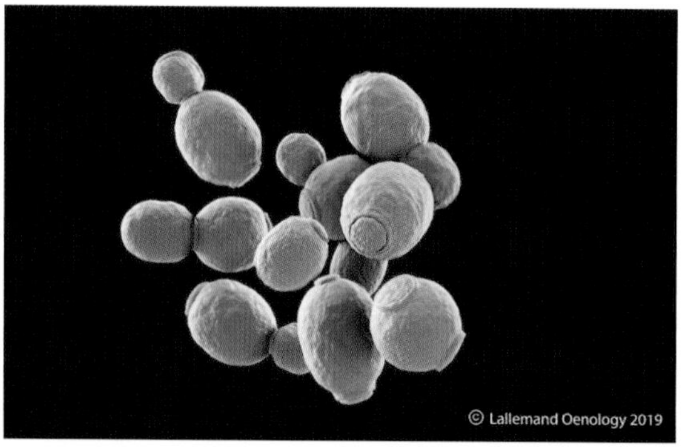

Yeast under the microscope.

A huge amount of CO_2 will be produced during the process and this should be remembered wherever the fermentation takes place, as it can be extremely dangerous in a tight space.

Nutrients

Growing grapes in a cool climate often means that they can be low in nitrogen. If they are, you will need to add some nitrogen during the alcoholic fermentation. Any hints of egg or 'off' aromas should be dealt with immediately. This eggy aroma is hydrogen sulphide (H_2S), caused by a lack of nitrogen. It is often easily rectified if nutrients are added early, as the fermentation will clean up and there will be no detrimental effect on the wine. If left too long, however, the H_2S can develop into mercaptans that are difficult to remove and will definitely have a negative effect on the finished product.

Monitoring the fermentation is the key to success and to rectifying any potential problems as fast as possible. Nutrients to add can be in the form of *diammonium phosphate* (DAP), or organic versions

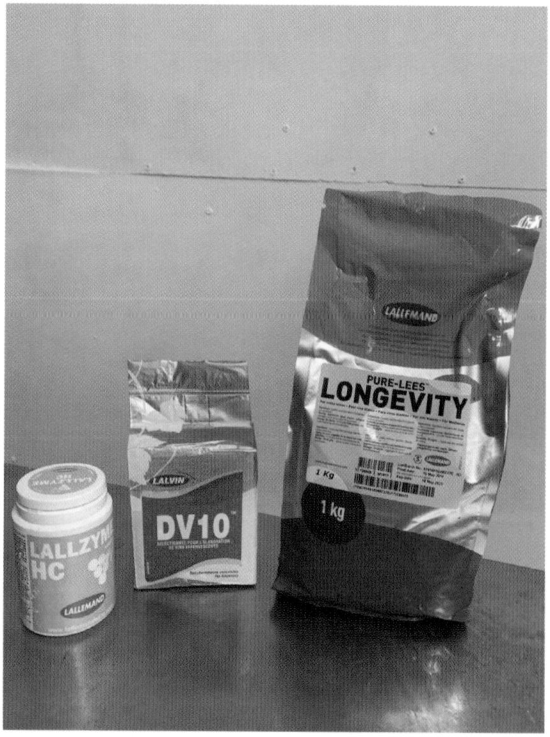

Basic wine-making supplies – yeast, enzyme and nutrient.

of the same product that are rich in nutrients, often derived from yeast hulls. If possible, source good-quality organic nutrients, as this creates a better environment for the juice and can promote aromas.

If you detect H_2S in the finished wine, it is too late to add nutrients and you will need to seek another solution. The following options may help to resolve the issue:

- Get your wine to 50ppm SO_2, rack the fully fermented wine and splash it around in the process. This may simply blow off the H_2S aroma and turn the H_2S back to elemental sulphur, which simply drops out. Racking two or three times should solve a mild case of H_2S, but be careful not to overdo it, as every time the wine is moved, it will bring more oxygen into the liquid. Also, if there are mercaptans present, this can oxidize those mercaptans, causing an even harder issue to resolve. Mercaptans are responsible for the odour of the skunk, but are also associated with onion, rubber, rotten eggs and cabbage.[8]
- A second method is to add copper – a reason why many older wineries had copper taps and fittings. This copper would turn the H_2S into copper sulphide, which would drop out of the wine. If you are making the wine on a microscale, simply adding copper coins may do the trick (this is also an impressive party trick when rectifying a wine that previously was displaying eggy smells). If you are operating on a large scale, there are several copper solution products that have the same effect. Again, follow manufacturers' advice and trial the process by adding the minimal amount at all times.

By monitoring the ferment and adding nutrient as required, these problems should be kept to a minimum.

MLF

You should now be considering whether or not you are going to put your wines through a malolactic fermentation (MLF). You should match your MLF bacterium with the pH of the wine to ensure that you have success. Too low a pH (under 3pH) can often mean that your options are far fewer than if your pH is over 3.1. Once you have carried out a pH test, choose your strain of bacterium and go for it.

Traditionally, MLF was carried out directly after the initial fermentation and for wine makers opting for a natural production procedure, the wine is left to carry out this process on its own. There are, however, certain strains of MLF bacteria that are best added during the initial fermentation stage; this works well because the tanks are naturally warm due to the fermentation and the perfect environment for an MLF. Further exploration into fermentation, including MLF, is included in Chapter 7.

Bâtonnage and Barrels

Bâtonnage is the process of stirring the lees to create wines with greater depth of flavour. It is most famously associated in the use of Chardonnay, but can be employed equally as well in many cool-climate grape varietals. Importantly, if you are going to employ bâtonnage you must make sure that you avoid oxidizing the wine in the process. How often you should carry out this procedure is really down to experience. There are wine makers who do it vigorously and often two to three times a week at the end of fermentation, while others believe that over-stirring can lead to a reduction in finesse in the finished wine and a diminished shelf life, so would be more cautious about the amount of stirring. If you do opt for bâtonnage, it will, in most circumstances, lead to greater depth and flavours in your wine.

ROSÉ WINE

Producing rosé is a similar process to white wine making. If making rosé in a traditional way (that is, not blending red and white wine), the main differences are that you will be using red grapes. The type of grape and how you press it are what will give you more – or less – colour.

The colour of rosé that you produce as a wine maker with basic kit is going to be decided by a few different factors. First, the varietal – if you have a thick-skinned variety, the colour will be darker than if you have a thinner-skinned variety.

A variety like Rondo, for example, pressed in the same way as a Pinot Noir will lead to very different results. Rondo will always produce more colour than a Pinot Noir, so if you desire a light-hued finished wine you will have to blend with a white wine later in the process.

Second, the colour will be affected by how hard the fruit is pressed and this is where it can be quite tricky for the wine maker with basic kit. The process will need to be controlled by visually checking the colour of the juice as it leaves the press. If you have a crusher/destemmer, this process on a gentle setting can allow the fruit to have just enough extra skin contact to give a nice rosé colour. Finally, the ripeness of the fruit will also decide how much colour is extracted; the greater the ripeness, the deeper the colour.

Fermenting in old oak barrels with a bubbler – micro-oxidation is the goal with these barrels to create soft, rounded flavours.

Bâtonnage to increase mouth feel in barrel-fermented wines.

Once the fruit has been pressed and you are dealing with the juice, rosé can be handled in exactly the same way as white wine, with the main factors to consider being aroma and maintenance of colour. It is crucial that the wine is exposed to the minimal amount of oxygen at all times so as to prevent browning, which affects the colour.

A historically non-traditional but accepted way of producing rosé is to blend white wine with red wine to provide the desired colour, flavour and aroma. This method means that you have control over your end product and will allow for greater complexity in the finished wine. Producing rosé in this style also gives the winemaker more control over total production output, meaning that he or she can have exactly the required number of each type of wine in bottle.

RED WINE

Red wine production follows a slightly different process to making white or rosé wines, with the main variance being that before the juice heads to the press it goes through a further procedure. On receiving the fruit, the grapes go through the crusher and destemmer, ending up with destalked grapes in an open-topped fermenting vessel. A consideration for the wine maker is whether you want to cold-macerate your grape juice. Cold maceration can lead to fruitier wines, yet the decision to do this or not can often be guided by the quality and cleanliness of the fruit. If there is any sign of disease, cold maceration is not a course of action to be recommended as it can encourage unwanted bacteria.

Before considering any additions, you need to know what the sugar and acid levels are and to make the appropriate additions now, prior to adding yeast. The next stage is the enzyme and yeast addition. The purpose of the enzyme is to break down the grape skins, releasing more juice. After the addition of the enzyme, you can then proceed to yeast addition. The yeast should be chosen based on its suitability to the fruit and the style of wine that you wish to make.

In cooler-climate wine making, it is better to try to produce a style that is most suited to the climate. In an exceptional year, this may be akin to a Burgundian red wine, but in an average year it is often best to try to achieve a style that is suited to the inherent qualities and varietal characteristic of your crop.

Make certain that your vessel has space for the fermentation to take place. As the fermentation proceeds the grape skins will rise up, so you will require about 15 per cent space in your tanks to prevent the juice and skins from overflowing.

As soon as you have grapes in your vessel, you can begin the process of punching down using a paddle (or similar), or pumping over by using a pump. Beware of pumping over as it can introduce too much oxygen into the wines and is difficult to regulate. Punching down tends to allow more control and ensures that the grape skins that have formed a cap can become completely submerged into the fermenting juice, aiding the extraction of colour and flavour.

Punch down should occur three times daily; morning, noon and night. At the very minimum you can get away with two punch downs. This process is designed for the juice to pick up colour and tannin from the grape skins during fermentation and to redistribute fermenting juice in the tank. A warmer fermentation (due to the grape skins forming a cap) leads to more colour extraction. Ideal temperatures for red wine fermentation are mid 20°C – warm enough to extract colour, whilst retaining aromatics in the juice/wines. Remember, at this temperature the fermentation will be much quicker than when producing white and rosé wines, so do not be surprised if the fermentation is completed in under a week.

It is very important to monitor continuously the ferment so that you know when it will finish. Once the fermentation does end and there is no remaining sugar, then the juice can be racked away through a racking valve or with a pump. The grapes should then be moved to the grape press to be pressed and the resulting liquid to be combined with the racked wine.

Once all of the wine has been extracted and racked into a new vessel, the wine should be monitored for the completion of alcoholic fermentation plus MLF. If the wines have completed both, they should receive an SO_2 addition of 40ppm and go into a further vessel for maturation. This could be oak barrels or stainless steel, depending on the desired outcome. Now follow the process as you would for white wine.

CHAPTER 7

FERMENTATION

Stainless-steel tanks with temperature control at Defined Wine in Kent.

Fermentation and the various stages surrounding it have been touched on already in Chapter 6. However, this section of the book will outline each area in more detail.

OPPOSITE: **Yeast about to be pitched into the juice.**

YEAST

Fermentation in wine making is the conversion of grape juice with high sugar content into alcohol and carbon dioxide. This is achieved through yeast, with the most-used commercial yeast being *Saccharomyces cerevisiae*. This yeast has been cultivated from the indigenous yeasts of vineyards in wine-producing regions around the world. By cultivating yeasts from known vineyards, it becomes possible to match yeast types with the fruit that is grown, meaning that you can buy a yeast that should provide a consistent result, which is very helpful when producing wine commercially.

As already mentioned, working with the fruit and respecting varietal character are the most important factors, especially in a cool climate. In a hot summer, the varietal may be more ripe and suited to a yeast that will produce wines that are fruitier in style for still wine. In cooler years, the same grape variety may be more suited to a sparkling wine style and therefore the yeast chosen should be different.

Producers of 'natural' wines will not add any yeast at all and will rely upon the yeasts that naturally occur on the fruit itself to put the wines through fermentation. This can lead to higher levels of glycerol, which is associated with greater mouthfeel and texture to a wine. There is, however, a risk involved in using a non-*Saccharomyces cerevisiae* yeast, as it may not have the capability to finish a fermentation fully, meaning that there is a higher likelihood of fermentation stoppages and failure. It also makes consistent results harder to achieve as you do not know what yeast will be fermenting the juice, but also as the fermentation proceeds it is not clear what yeast will finish a fermentation. In a commercial winery with larger-scale production, this could produce unreliable results.

TEMPERATURE

The temperature at which you ferment the juice will have a big impact on the finished wine, with different

Ideal small vessels for the primary fermentation.

temperatures of fermentation leading to very different results. It was believed by many wine makers that cooler temperatures may lead to fruitier wines and this has been known with some yeast strains to be the case, but is not true for all strains. It is best to follow the recommended fermentation temperatures, as yeast does not like ultra-cool fermentations and these may lead to problematic and stuck fermentations.

When it comes to temperature control, absolute regulation can only be achieved with temperature-controlled tanks, chiller unit and thermostat, which requires a considerable investment. Having said this, wine makers working on a budget have been known to rig up a system where cold water is allowed to run on to a fermenting tank to cool it. This does work and can cool a hot fermentation – which can be very useful.

It is also not uncommon for ice in bags to be put into a tank to chill it, but this is more problematic, as ultimately the juice will be changing temperature rapidly from hot to cool and would lead to results that would be difficult to log and ultimately replicate. Nevertheless, if this is the only option versus a hot fermentation for white wines – that is, over 25°C – then ice cubes in bags are a necessity.

Successful white wines with full aromas and flavour often benefit from a cool fermentation at around 12–14°C. This has become popular thanks to the very expressive Sauvignon Blanc being produced in New Zealand and other cooler-climate makers wanting to replicate their success. At these temperatures, you should expect fruitier wines, but use a good nutrient regime to ensure that the yeast does not stop working and to achieve the best flavour profile.

In red wine production, temperature is still important, but for rather different reasons. As noted in Chapter 6, red wines are fermented on their skins and when the skins separate from the juice it forms a cap. The cap rises to the top of the fermentation vessel, where it has the effect of keeping the juice warmer and impeding oxygen. By warming the juice, it means that the juice extracts more colour (in the same way as if you were making a cup of tea – the greater colour comes from warmer temperatures). The cap also impedes oxygen that can produce 'off' flavours in the fermenting juice – a key reason why you need to have a robust punch-down/pump-over regime in place, or your wine could end up with unwanted aromas.

The ideal temperature for red wine making is in the region of 22–29°C. At this temperature, you will have very happy yeast that will ferment the sugar well.

Whist the red wine is fermenting and the temperatures are over 20°C, it is best practice – as in white wine making – to monitor the sugar depletion rates with a hydrometer and also to take the temperature of the juice. This will allow you control and give an insight into what is happening and, crucially, what is going to happen next.

As the fermentation starts to slow down and the yeast runs out of fermentable sugars, the temperature will begin to drop. When your fermenting juice nears the stage where it reads 1.000 specific gravity (SG), you should be thinking about separating the juice from the skins and pressing what is left. However, some wine makers will leave the skins in contact with the juice for an extended period after fermentation has ceased to try to give more character to the wines, although this can lead to a stewed character in the wine.

As the wine reaches 1.000 SG, it is recommended to separate the juice and then press the remainder of the skins. This can be a messy business, so have a plan in place as to how you are going to achieve this. Once you have pressed off the skins and all of the juice/wine is in the same tank, you can monitor the end of the fermentation. This should see the hydrometer read in the region of 0.990–0.995 SG. Once you are down at these figures and have been there for a few days you know that your fermentation has finished. The wine should start to clarify on its own and it is time to add SO_2 to stabilize.

MALOLACTIC FERMENTATION

In cool-climate wine making, a malolactic fermentation (MLF) is a good process to put your wines through. The MLF softens the wine and changes the acidity from malic acid (green apple) to lactic acid (yogurt), meaning that it noticeably softens the wine whilst adding complexity and making it more textural.

MLF will occur spontaneously most of the time if the wines are left to do their own thing and are over 3.3pH

Barrels are an ideal environment to encourage an MLF.

and in the absence of SO_2. The bacterium oenococcus oeni carries out the conversion, by changing and decarboxylating the malic acid to lactic. It is not actually a 'fermentation' in the traditional sense, but it does produce CO_2 and as such it does make your wine safe whilst the MLF is on-going. This means that the wine maker does not have to worry so much about potential wine spoilage.

There are different ways of conducting an MLF, either by *co-inoculating* with the juice right at the start of fermentation, or by adding it to the wines after primary fermentation has finished. MLF can reduce the acidity by up to 2g/l, whilst also adding beneficial texture to the finished wine. Therefore, if you are making wine in a cooler climate, it is a great tool for reducing acid. It also keeps the wines in far better balance than if you put them through a chemical de-acidification.

Whilst lots of producers of cool-climate wines are very protective of the acids in their juice and wine – and quite rightly so, as the acids are often the hallmark of the wines – remember that in the world of wine, the UK does have high acid and by putting wines with 10g/l upwards through MLF, it is not going to produce 'flabby' wines. There are still going to be good levels of acid to give the wine structure and to allow the MLF to improve the wines.

One of the criticisms of MLF is that it turns wines 'creamy', producing *diacetyl*. This should not be the case unless you opt for bacteria that are specifically designed to do this – and they do exist. These bacteria will produce butter and cream flavours that can be a nice textural component within wines, but, when overdone, can be cloying and put the wine out of balance. There are, however, plenty of commercial bacteria that produce extremely low levels of diacetyl. The timing of the addition of bacteria can also affect the level of diacetyl. The more experience you have of adding bacteria, the more you will understand what works for your wine. Choose a bacterium that suits the wine's pH levels. Understand what it is being used to do. Is it designed just to reduce acidity, or is the aim to give creamy, buttery flavours in your wines? Knowing this will lead to the correct bacterium being chosen.

You must also understand the temperature your wine needs to be at in order to undergo MLF successfully. If it requires 14+°C, you will need a way to warm up the tank or vessel. By co-inoculating the wines with the yeast, you can actually put wines through MLF faster than if you add the bacterium once fermentation has finished. Often overlooked and yet very important is MLF nutrient. The bacterium has certain nutrient requirements that need addressing; make sure that you add these at the start of the MLF to ensure that you do not have any issues over the fermentation period.

Once you think that the MLF has ended or is near completion, use chromatography paper to find out. This is a simple test by which you compare the wine's acidity to that of malic acid. These kits are easy to obtain and to use and will give you quick results to find out if you have successfully carried out an MLF. Once MLF is completed – and assuming that your primary fermentation is also complete – you can rack off your wine and stabilize.

STABILITY – SO_2/PROTEIN STABILITY/COLD STABILITY

It is crucial to have control over SO_2, protein stability and cold, or tartrate, stability – if any of these three elements are not taken care of, it will lead to failure for the producer.

Too low a quantity of SO_2 will mean that the wine will most likely have a shorter shelf life and there is a higher chance of *brettanomyces* (*brett*) developing. Brett can lead to the 'pet shop' flavour that is commonly referred to in wine tasting as 'mousiness'. In fact, brett used to be far rarer, but since more wine makers are now seeking to make wines with minimal SO_2, the taste is becoming ever more common. Protein stability is crucial, as, if not achieved, it can lead to a swirling haze developing in the finished wine, which is definitely not a good appearance. Cold, or tartrate, stability is required, or else tartrates will form in the wine and, although these tartrates do not affect the flavour, they will definitely affect the consumer appeal of the wines.

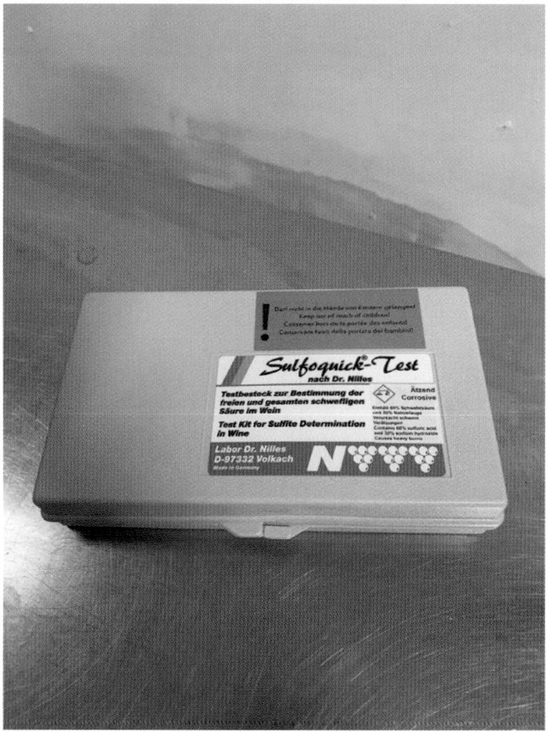

Portable SO_2 testing kit using the ripper method.

All of these stability factors are quite straightforward to deal with, but need to be rectified and checked before going into bottle.

SO_2 Stability

Let's deal firstly with SO_2. Sulphur dioxide is a chemical that prevents wine from oxidizing; it also prevents spoilage and will keep your wines tasting and smelling as they should. It is naturally produced during every fermentation in low levels and adding more is not to be feared. However, too much SO_2 can be potentially hazardous and can make wine undrinkable, so it is vital to know what you are doing and have the correct PPE when handling this substance.

Free and Bound SO_2

The element of SO_2 that actually protects the wine is free SO_2. As the wine is exposed to oxygen this free element decreases and becomes bound SO_2, that is, it is bound in the wine, but no longer providing protection from oxygen or bacteria. This is when you need to monitor SO_2 levels throughout the maturation period and maintain free levels of SO_2 at a level suited to the pH of the wine. When free and bound SO_2 are combined, this is known as total SO_2; keep careful watch of how much you add and monitor the total levels throughout the process.

SO_2 Levels

When you start to process the fruit, add 40ppm SO_2 at the press or crush. Do not add any more SO_2 now until after fermentation is complete. Following fermentation, the wine is very secure as it is still on the ferment lees, which naturally contain SO_2 and also the lees consume oxygen. If you are putting your wines through an MLF, you want them at 15ppm free SO_2 or less, then following MLF it is best to mature wines at 40ppm free SO_2 to ensure that they are safe from oxidation and spoilage.

It is best practice to check these SO_2 levels on at least a monthly basis. Every time the wine is moved, you should be aiming for 40ppm afterwards. The only time that this is not the case is when you are preparing wines for sparkling production, as ideally the wine should be under 15ppm SO_2 or lower as you put the wines through the secondary fermentation.

As touched on in Chapter 6, the equation that is used to work out how much SO_2 to add is:

- 1g SO_2 = 10ppm @1hl

Therefore, to secure a barrel of wine assuming the barrel is 225l, the equation is worked as follows:

- 1g SO_2 = 10ppm @1hl
- 2.2g SO_2 = 10ppm @2.2hl

We want 40ppm, therefore:

- 8.8g SO_2 = 40ppm @2.2hl

If we are using PMS that is half the strength of SO_2, so we double the 8.8g:

- 8.8g × 2 = 17.6g

Protein Stability and Fining

Wine has a high protein content, which, if left unchecked, will cause a haze to form. Adding a fining agent will lead to clearer wines. However, be wary of over-fining your wine, as this will cause a loss of aroma and flavour. If you are fining at any levels other than the minimum, you should be conducting fining trials to find out what is the minimum quantity that can be used.

There is a host of different fining products that can be used, such as bentonite, egg white, casein and isinglass. Bentonite is the focus here, as it works effectively on both red and white wine and is vegan-friendly and easy to handle. Bentonite is an absorptive, negatively charged powder, which, when mixed with water, becomes clay that works by attracting the positive protein particles in wine and juice. Once the clay is added it works very quickly and the protein and sediment drops to the bottom of the vessel. The clean wine or juice can then be racked off, leaving behind the unwanted sediment.

To prepare the bentonite, it needs to be mixed with warm water and then given at least twenty-four hours before adding it to the juice or wine, to give the slurry a better opportunity to expand and to be more effective. It should be added to juice at a rate of between 10 and 25g/hl; if you are adding it to wine, ensure that you carry out trials to ascertain the lowest possible addition. Once you have added the bentonite and given the solution at least a one-week period to settle, the wine can be racked into a fresh tank.

It is possible to check if you have achieved protein stability by a relatively straightforward test. Place 25ml of a clean sample (ideally filtered) into a watertight container and heat it in an 80°C water bath for a six-hour period. After the six-hour period, leave the sample to cool for three hours. If, when the sample has cooled, no haze has developed, the wine can be considered protein-stable.

Cold Stability

If a wine is not made cold-stable before bottling, it can lead to tartrate crystals dropping out of the

A long tartrate crystal in a bottle of sparkling wine. This will have to be double- or even triple-disgorged to remove.

wine – which can be off-putting to those drinking the wine, as it looks as if you have a snow globe inside of your wine bottle! If producing sparkling wine, tartrates can lead to gushing and overly agitated wine, which will negatively affect your reputation as a producer.

If you are making wine at home and it is not a commercial product, you may decide you are not concerned about the presence of tartrates. However, if you are selling to the general public, you will need to address this and, fortunately, it is a relatively easy thing to remedy. Simply maturing the wines outside on a number of the coldest consecutive nights of the year should achieve the aim; any tartrates will drop during this process. It has to be colder outside than any fridge environment, or it will only give your wines partial cold stability.

For wine making on a bigger scale, you will undoubtedly need to invest in equipment to aid this process, including double-insulated cooling jackets on wine tanks, ideally with a thermostat built in so that you can control the temperatures on each tank. You will also require a chilling unit with glycol storage, so as to be able to bring the wine down to −1°C. If wines are kept down at that temperature for a two- to three-week period, you will have achieved cold stabilization for your wine and can then start to rack it. When racking any wine that is still in a cold state, remember that it can pick up about twice as much oxygen than when it is at room temperature, so ensure that all tanks and hoses are purged with inert gas prior to any wine movement.

If you send your wines off for analysis and the result comes back that they are not cold-stable, there are solutions you can buy to remedy this. Carboxymethyl cellulose (CMC) will prevent tartrate crystals from dropping out of the wine and make it cold-stable. The only caveat is that the wine must be protein-stable before you add the CMC, or it can react negatively and drop a haze.

RACKING

The timing of racking is hugely important to your wines being as good as they can be, and not just from a clarity perspective – as it is possible to rack your wines clear enough for commercial clarity – but, more importantly, for flavour. If you fail to rack your wines, you will most

Racking between tanks to obtain clear juice or wine.

likely end up with a lot of the flavour of the lees; depending on your lees, this could add mouthfeel and be a good move. However, if those lees are not spot on, it is more likely that you will bring in unclean 'green' flavours into your finished wines, such as cabbage and even onion.

The first rack should be carried out twenty-four hours after pressing the grapes. This gives the maximum beneficial time for the lees to drop out of the juice. Once you have racked, you can then start the primary fermentation.

Following the completion of primary fermentation, it is recommended to rack again, depending on the quality of the lees. If the lees taste good, the wine can stay in contact longer. During this racking there is more flexibility, as keeping the wine on its ferment lees can lead to the more enhanced flavours already referred to. It is not unknown to leave wine on the lees for several months if good quality.

The ferment lees also give more protection in the wine, as the dead yeast cells safeguard it from spoilage and oxidation. However, a note of caution; for this to be successful, you need really good lees, which taste clean and/or smell fresh, as you do not want unripe flavours in your finished wine.

CLARIFICATION

Following the completion of fermentation and MLF, wines will start to clarify on their own. If this occurs more slowly than you may want, you can also consider filtration as a means of clarifying. However, do ensure that the wines are stable before filtration, so as to avoid having to filter twice. The filtration process requires you to charge the filter with wine and this process may lead to a loss of wine – therefore if dealing with smaller quantities take extra care.

For wine making over 500l, the filtration options are a pad and paper filter, a diatomaceous earth (DE) filter or – if you have a bigger budget – a crossflow filter. All filters, if handled well, will do a good job. More often than not, the issues tend to arise from a lack of operator experience, as opposed to any fundamental flaw with the equipment.

Diatomaceous earth filter – a great filter for handling an array of liquids, but which requires plenty of practice to become efficient in its use.

There are a couple of key things that you must do to ensure successful filtration. First, you need to clean and sanitize your machine thoroughly before use. Filters are a seasonal item and can therefore be left idling for a good few months before they are used again, so will always require a good clean. You must also make sure that you have the correct machine for the task that you are asking it to do. The crossflow filter will filter your wines to sterile on the first go, but you must ensure that you know how to do it. A crossflow filter is an expensive item, so you need to be producing in the region of at least 20,000l+ to justify this piece of kit.

DE filters are less expensive, but still a considerable financial commitment for a small winery. They allow the producer to handle a wider array of solids in the liquid and, once you have purchased the machine, it is actually cheaper per filter run than the less expensive pad filters over the longer term. Once you have got a good handle on how to use a DE filter (it can take quite a lot of practice), you can also push through any liquid with inert gasses such as CO_2 or nitrogen.

If you do not fancy getting to grips with a DE filter and are small-batch filtering, there are some decent small pad filters available. These filters perform poorly if the wine is not clear, so it is important that you have racked and fined your wine before this stage.

ACHIEVING STERILITY IN BOTTLED WINE

If you are using a DE filter or small pad filter, a cartridge filter will be needed to catch any powder or particles that are bigger than 1micron (μ). 1μ is important as that is the approximate size of yeast particles and will ensure that no wild yeast can enter the wine. After the catch, you can move to the membrane filter (0.45μ–0.65μ). This filter will catch any long-rod bacteria and should be protected as much as possible, as the membrane filter cartridge is expensive. Following the membrane filter, you can proceed to your bottling machine and bottle. You must ensure that anything that will come into contact with the wine has been sterilized; this is best achieved through steam or using peracetic acid (*see* Chapter 6).

Once you have sterilized the line it is important never to break the chain in hoses between the catch filter, membrane filter and bottle machine. It is the membrane filter that guarantees you sterility, so this is the key item in the chain – do not break the line beyond this point. Also, note that when cleaning and sterilizing the cartridges make sure that you bring your PAA, steam and hot water out of the top point of the

Microbiological dip-slide testing can be used to let you know if any yeast or bacteria is in your wine – on this slide something is alive!

A steamer is a great bit of kit for sterilizing vessels and bottling lines; just ensure that all parts receive the steam.

cartridge. There should be a valve on top of this filter that will allow liquid or steam out.

PAA is a sterilizer and not a cleaning chemical, so use it in conjunction with a good clean. Cleaning is best carried out with caustic soda or enzymatic cleaners that are designed to break down solids. Ensure that any alkaline cleaner has been thoroughly flushed with water before using PAA. You can buy pH strips that will give you an instant result and are very cost-effective. Ensure that the PAA or steam hits every part of the bottling machine and that you bring the solution through the filling heads.

BOTTLING

Once you have achieved sterility with your line and the wine is bright and clear, you can proceed to the bottling stage. If you have done everything correctly up to this point, it should be relatively straightforward, as there is nothing that can block the wine en route to the bottling machine.

When you bring the wine in, ensure that it takes up all the space in the cartridge filter; this improves the lifespan of these cartridges and the speed at which bottling can take place. Make sure that there are no leakages anywhere in the system and that everything is sound, especially beyond the membrane filter.

Bottles, if purchased from a quality bottling company, will arrive sterile. However, as they are stored upright, there may be instances where foreign objects have come into the bottle, so it is advisable to rinse bottles prior to bottling. If your water source does not contain a sterile filter, then – again – you need to guarantee that the bottles are sterile. This is best done

Bottling machine in action.

with PAA, SO_2 or citric acid. If using PAA, make sure that there is no residue in the bottle prior to filling it, or it may oxidize the wine.

If using corks, make sure that you always use a fresh packet of corks each season and always store them in dry conditions, as cork can pick up moulds that will ruin your wine. After all of this effort and time put into making your wine, it would be devastating to be pouring it away due to any last-minute failures. The bottom line with packaging is that everything must be clean and sterilized and if you can prove and log your cleaning and sterility systems, there is far less likelihood of issues arising.

CHAPTER 8

SPARKLING WINE PRODUCTION – TRADITIONAL METHOD

English sparkling wine is one of the most exciting products available to consumers today. This comes down to the fruit being grown in the UK that's best suited to sparkling wine production being very similar – and arguably superior – to our nearest quality wine-producing region in Champagne. As the climate gets warmer, we should see wines improving year on year and improved yields, making English sparkling wine not only a quality product, but potentially a highly profitable one. This chapter focuses on the stages of sparkling wine production, from primary fermentation through to the final product.

English sparkling wine being enjoyed at a trade tasting.

OPPOSITE: **Sparkling wine on a pupitre being riddled.**

Following primary fermentation, once the wine is cold- and protein-stable – plus any sediment has been removed either by careful racking or filtration – the wine is now ready to undergo secondary fermentation. Before commencing the secondary fermentation, the base wine should tick a number of boxes in its production:

- The wine itself should have SO_2 levels below 15ppm, or it may make fermentation in the bottle problematic. Ideally, there should be as little SO_2 as possible in the wine at this stage without the wines being at risk of spoilage.
- Preferably the wine should be filtered to avoid large quantities of sediment dropping out at a later date. Remember – if you have not got the ability to filter wines, careful racking can also be very effective; just ensure that all movements are carried out as vigilantly as possible and ideally with inert gas.
- Sterile filtering of the wines is advised to ensure that no MLF bacteria are left in the bottle, as an MLF occurring at the same time as a secondary fermentation is undesirable.
- The base wine needs to be fermented to dryness during the initial fermentation, or it could result in too much sugar being available during the secondary fermentation.
- The base wine needs to be cold-stable. Cold stability will ensure that your wines will not produce any tartrate crystals as time progresses, either whilst ageing or after *riddling* and *disgorging*. It is also worth bearing in mind that cold-stability tests often test wine to around 2°C, therefore if you are storing your wines in colder temperatures than this, the wine can still drop tartrates. Refer to carboxymethyl cellulose in Chapter 7, which can be used to stabilize the wines. If you do get tartrates in your bottles during the secondary fermentation it is possible (but difficult) to remove them in the riddling process, but it takes a lot of effort shaking the bottles to get the crystals to a manageable size where they can be riddled into the neck of the bottle and ultimately disgorged.
- The wines also need to be protein-stable prior to any bottling. Do not be drawn into a debate about wines needing proteins to retain bubbles. While this is true, the secondary fermentation will allow for sufficient protein in the wine so that the bubbles will retain in the glass once poured.

Acids for sparkling wines should be in the range of 8–12TA and 2.9–3.2pH. These are ideal parameters. It is worth considering the use of chemical and biological means to bring your base wine back into these ranges if they are outside. This can be a procedure such as MLF or de-acidification products.

The ideal range for base wine ABV is between 10–11.5 per cent. If less than this, the wine would benefit from being chaptalized up to 10–10.5 per cent. However, remember that chaptalization is subject to rules and regulations. In a 'normal' UK year, wines can be chaptalized up to 3 per cent ABV. Any more alcohol than 11.5 per cent and – combined with acidity being lower than 8TA – it can lead to 'flabby' wines. Structure and acid are crucial in the final product, providing the framework for the secondary fermentation to hang from.

When pressing the juice, it needs to be done softly – ideally a cuvée – up to 0.8bar pressure at the press and no more than 51 per cent of juice extracted. This is probably the most important part of the whole process. If you are pressing for cuvée-only wines, consider what you can do with the remainder of the juice that could be extracted. Should you press harder and make another style of sparkling wine, or simply press off and use this juice as a blending tool? There are several options – the most important thing is planning.

For a winery or smaller production, MLF can be the preferred option because of its ability to soften acids whilst making the wine more complex and at the same time protecting it whilst it releases CO_2. If the winery is hygienic and correct protocols have been followed, the wine can spend longer without SO_2 additions and will be further protected by the MLF process.

A gentle whole-bunch press is ideal for the production of quality sparkling wine.

BLENDING

This is your chance to put your own stamp on the wines. This could be a blend of the press fractions from the same wine, or it could be a blend of different varieties, or a blend of the same variety with different yeasts, or a blend of wines over a number of vintages. There is a lot of choice, but the key is to understand *why* you are doing everything that you do in the winery.

You should now be aware of the various components needed for wine making. *See* the table for the ideal parameters for successful sparkling wine.

Ideal Parameters for Successful Sparkling Wine

Juice

TA	8–12
pH	2.9–3.2
ABV (potential alcohol)	10–11%

Getting the ideal colour, aroma and flavour into the finished blend requires a lot of experience.

Pressing

Cuvée – 51% of tonnage	Up to 0.8bar
Taille	0.8–1.2bar
Hard pressing	1.2bar+
SO_2	40ppm addition

Fermentation

Pre-fermentation	• Settle for 24–48 hours
Finings	• Add finings to aid flocculation and create protein stability. Carry out this process as soon as possible – it has a more positive effect on the finished wine than any additions made later in the process
Enzyme	• Adding enzyme at the juice stage is recommended to increase the amount of clean juice
Rack	• When racking is complete, make any sugar additions so that the must is at the recommended level for 10–11% ABV

	• Ensure that the sugar is well homogenized into the juice or use liquid sugar • 17g/l = 1% increase in ABV
Ferment clean juice	• Use a sparkling wine-related yeast
Nutrients	• Add according to instructions • Generally ⅓ through fermentation, then ⅔ through fermentation • If any sign of H_2S, up your nutrient regime
MLF	• Less than 3.1pH classic sparkling wine bateria developed in the Champagne region to de-acidify acidic wines cannot be used in a co-inoculation • More than 3.1pH you can co-inoculate, saving you money; often this MLF will only take 7–14 days to complete • SO_2 less than 15ppm free

Post-fermentation

Rack and stabilize	• Post-fermentation and MLF – rack the wines; ideally do this at a controlled and slow pump speed • Now that you have made base wine, oxidation becomes a key factor; if possible, use CO_2 or nitrogen to protect the wine from oxygen at all times • SO_2 at this stage to be raised to 40ppm
Cold stabilize	• Cold-stabilize – drop the wine to –2°C for 14–21-day period
Filter	• Filter the wines under a blanket of CO_2/nitrogen
Blending	• Taste-test and trial all wines – put together a panel of tasters if possible to give a broad range of opinion
Test	• Check cold stability is stable • Check protein stability is stable • Check SO_2 is ideally 15ppm or less • Check ABV is 10–11.5%
Bottling	• If all is in range and the wines are stable, clean and filtered, you can now bottle your wines

SECONDARY FERMENTATION

Yeast starter culture being established.

Tirage

Tirage is the process of starting secondary fermentation. It is important to decide how much pressure you want in the bottle. The table correlates sugar additions to the required pressure. This is an indicator of how much sugar will be required, depending on levels of alcohol in the base wine.

Correlation of Sugar Additions and Pressure

Desired Pressure / ABV %	5bar	5.5bar	6bar
9%	19g/l	21g/l	23g/l
10%	20g/l	22g/l	24g/l
11%	21g/l	23g/l	25g/l
12%	22g/l	24g/l	26g/l

Preparation

To start the secondary fermentation process, it is necessary to build up the mother culture for the wine, otherwise it is unlikely that the wine will go through the process successfully.

First, you have to pick the correct yeast strain and this is where you should choose a *Saccharomyces bayanus* (SB) strain as opposed to *Saccharomyces cerevisiae* (SC). *Saccharomyces bayanus* is a stronger fermenter in difficult conditions and there can be fewer

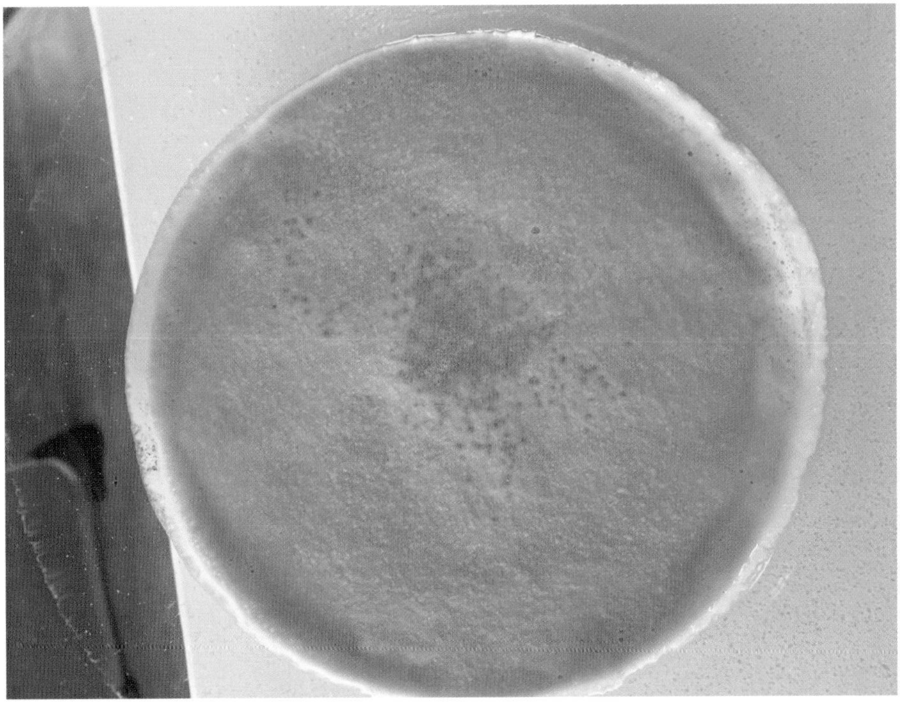

Yeast culture after twenty minutes; do not stir in the first twenty minutes so that the yeast cell walls remain intact.

more difficult conditions in a bottle than no oxygen, high alcohol to start with and some SO_2 in the bottle. The SB yeast strain should have relatively low nitrogen requirements and can ferment at reasonably low temperatures.

Unless base wine is stored in temperature-controlled conditions, it is likely that the wine in bottle is going to be below 10°C and it is highly recommended that the wine be no less than this temperature when commencing the fermentation. Ideally, it would be in the region of 15°C, which is a reason why spring is a good time to start the wines on the secondary fermentation process.

With the correct quantity of sugar and yeast strain chosen, you can move on to building up the mother culture – the fermenting yeast culture that is strong enough to withstand difficult fermenting conditions. It takes a number of days for this culture to be of the required strength and to be budding at the correct speed.

Secondary Fermentation based on 1,000l of Wine

Step 1 Rehydrate the Yeast – Fifteen Minutes

Rehydrate the yeast using water with added nutrient. Add the water and nutrient mix at 43°C. When the temperature drops to 35°C, slowly sprinkle the yeast on to the surface of the water–nutrient mix. Do not stir at this stage as it can damage the yeast cell wall.

Yeast–Water Proportions

Yeast (g)	160
Water (l) @ 35°C	1

Step 2 Make the Water–Sugar Mix

To ensure that the yeast really gets going, make up a water–sugar mix that will allow the yeast to multiply at a rapid rate. This mix should be a 50:50 mix of sugar and water. Remember to take into account weight in grams when it converts to liquid, as this conversion equates to the weight in grams multiplied by 0.6. So, for 500g of sugar, multiply by 0.6 and you get 300ml of liquid sugar. Therefore, for a 1l batch of sugar/water, mix 500g of sugar and 700ml of water. The water can be warmed up to allow the sugar to dissolve easily; it should then be allowed to stand to reach 20°C.

Starter – Day 1

Starter	Quantity
Water/yeast mix (l)	1
Base wine (l) 37°C	1
Water liquer (l) 37°C	1
Nutrient (g)	5

Step 3 Making the Starter – Eighteen to Twenty-Four Hours Later

The rehydrated yeast mix should be added to the liquer mix and the same quantity of still base wine. For 1,000l of wine total, the quantities can be found in the table. Nutrient should also be added to assist the yeast multiplication. The starting density of this mix should be 1.063SG. Temperature should be maintained at no lower than 20°C, or it simply will not be a favourable enough environment for the yeast.

The wine should be stirred or splashed to aerate and careful attention must be taken to ensure that the yeast is consuming the sugar at the required rate, so that in four to five days the starter mix is between 1.010 and 1.000 SG.

First Multiplication – Eighteen to Twenty-Four Hours Later

First Multiplication	Quantity
Starter mix (l)	3
Water (l) @ 37°C	12
Base wine (l)	12
Nutrient	5
Wine Liquer	
Sugar (kg)	9.6
Wine (l) 37°C	9.6
Total culture (l)	**42.34**

Step 4 – Day Four

Temperature is very important and should be maintained at 20°C.

Every morning and evening, stir and check the density. The mother – now starter – culture is ready to be used when the density is at 1.000SG. If the SG drops faster, it is possible to keep the culture active by adding a little more sugar.

The total sugar added is not particularly important; what is important is that the culture is active. If you have a microscope, yeast cells should be between 50–70 million cells.

With your starter culture made and multiplying at the correct rate, mix with the base wine. There should also be a combination of nutrients and riddling agents in the mix to ensure that the yeast is happy and that when you come to riddle and disgorge the wine, removing the yeast is as easy as possible.

Nutrients are added to minimize the risk of stuck fermentations, as the nutrients in the base wine have been depleted following primary fermentation.

Suggested Amount of Sugar, Nutrients and Riddling Agents Used to Produce 1,000l of Sparkling Wine

Day 4	Quantity
Yeast culture	42.34
Sugar (kg)	24
Riddling agent (ml)	715
Nutrient (ml)	204
Tannin (ml) (optional)	204
Mannoprotein (g) (optional)	255
Phosphate titres (G)	20

Once you have mixed this together you can proceed to bottling. There are a few crucial factors to remember and think about. First, the yeast culture must be strong and it must be viable, as it does not want to be 'shocked' as it moves on to the next stage of the process.

The strength of the culture can be judged by how efficiently it is consuming the sugar and its rate. If it is not consuming the sugar in the four days, you could try extra agitation, nutrient or warmth. Unless the yeast

Crown cap with in-built bidule to help with the disgorging process.

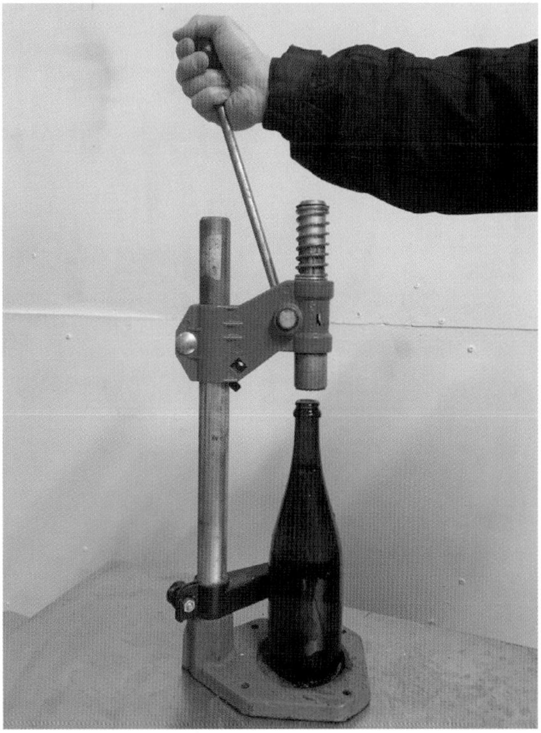

Crown capper machine for putting the corks on the bottle.

is not consuming the sugar, there is no need for more yeast; encouraging the culture you have got is the better option.

In small-batch sparkling wine making, ensure that you really homogenize the sugar mix, as any lumps of sugar could be enough for a wine bottle to explode, which could get messy, noisy and dangerous! In an ideal world you would have a way of permanently stirring this mix whilst you were bottling to ensure that it does mix successfully and there are not any lumps. In a commercial setting, some form of stirring device can be used that very effectively keeps the wine agitated whilst bottling. Ultimately, it is about you as a wine maker doing the best that you can to ensure a successful operation.

COMMON ISSUES AND RESOLUTIONS

Population of the yeast in the starter culture is too low If this occurs, it is often the result of not enough oxygenation at the multiplication phase and not enough nutrient being introduced.

Temperature is too cold for secondary fermentation Bottles should be stored at the correct temperature for yeast to be active; this is generally around 13°C. If it is too cold for the yeast, you run the risk of a failed secondary fermentation in bottle. This is the reason why spring/summer is the preferred time to carry out secondary fermentation in bottle.

Alcohol level is too high This is a result of too much sugar being added to the wine/sugar/water mix.

Free SO_2 level if too high prior to bottling Do not bottle if the free SO_2 is over 15ppm. If it is higher than 15ppm leading up to bottling try racking the wine and test again; this may bind up some of the free SO_2.

Starter culture has too much sugar Delay bottling and if you can, increase the temperature of the mother culture, then agitate. This will lead to a faster consumption of sugar. With small batches it is very easy to have too much sugar, which will cause bottles to explode, whilst too little is often disappointing for the consumer.

Starter culture is too dry as you approach bottling Check the yeast viability, make a complementary sugar addition and postpone bottling. All being well, you can then proceed to bottling when between 1.000 and 1.010SG.

TIME IN SECONDARY FERMENTATION

The time that the wine spends in secondary fermentation will have a direct influence on the complexity of the finished product. Current guidelines suggest a 'quality' sparkling wine should have at least

Bottles of secondary fermented wine going through the ageing process in a darkened room, ideal to avoid light strike.

twelve months' secondary fermentation time. However, twelve months is usually not long enough to transfer the complexity of the flavours of yeast degradation into a finished wine. If you are hoping to achieve greater complexity, it is advised that the wines need to age for at least two to three years in secondary, for these flavours to develop.

If, as the wine maker, you are trying to create a wine that is fruit-driven and without many of the flavours associated with autolysis (bread, biscuit, brioche and so on), the amount of time that the wine spends in secondary fermentation is not of as much importance.

Ensure that you do everything you can to store any wine in a dark space, as light can ruin the wine via a process called *light strike*, causing vegetal and unpleasant flavours. If you do not have a dark space, invest in some black shrinkwrap to cover up the bottles, as this will prevent light strike.

Sparkling wine that has been on a pupitre for at least three weeks of tilting and twisting.

Gyro-pallettes at a large commercial winery at Defined Wine in Kent.

RIDDLING

Following the ageing process, the next stage is riddling. Riddling is the removal of the dead yeast cells in the bottle. It is recommended to use a pupitre to carry out this process, or if you can spend a bit more, a gyro-pallette. To use a pupitre, the bottles start semi-inverted and are gradually tilted and twisted over a three-week period (at least) until all the sediment has slid into the neck of the bottle.

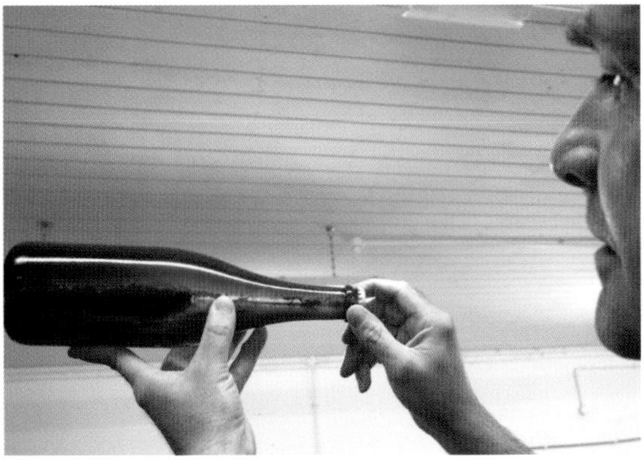

Inspecting the yeast in a bottle of sparkling wine before riddling at Polgoon Vineyard in Cornwall.

The bottles should be twisted in such a way as to encourage the yeast to dislodge and move down the neck. With each movement the bottle will gradually be tilted more and more upright until all the yeast is finally in the neck of the bottle and in the bidule that sits in the crown. The bidule is required to help form a plug with the yeast so that disgorging is a cleaner process.

DISGORGING

Following the riddling process, the wine is now ready to be disgorged. It is always recommended to wear safety goggles and protective gloves when handling bottles of sparkling wine during disgorging. It is also recommended to disgorge in cool winery conditions,

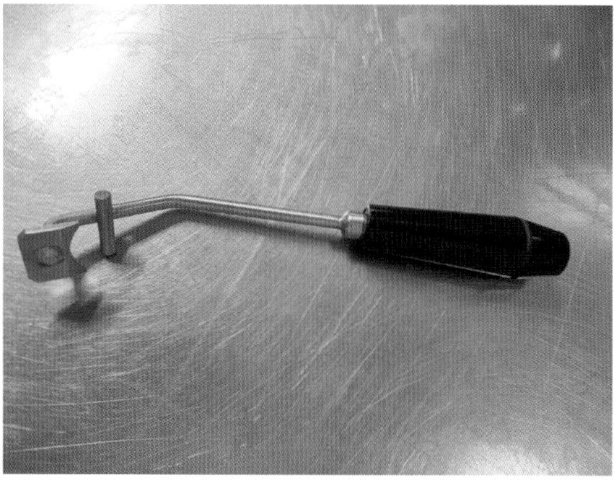

A disgorging key or inverted crown-cap remover is used to remove the crown cap on sparkling wine bottles.

so that the carbonated wine in the bottle does not become too agitated, as warm wine will behave very differently to cool wine.

The cleanest way of disgorging is by using a neck freezer, filled with glycol and water and chilled to around –20°C. The bottles are kept inverted and placed in the neck freezer. The portion of the bottle that contains the yeast should then be placed in the solution (around 2cm). After a short period of time, the yeast plug is frozen and the bottles can be handled without fear of disturbing the plugged sediment. A disgorging key is then used to remove the plug of yeast. This plug will be expelled due to the pressure of the wine behind the frozen portion of wine and the remaining wine should now be completely clear of yeast and ready for top-up and *dosage*.

If you do not have a neck freezer, the process of disgorging is similar, although requires more practice to perfect. With the wine bottle inverted, the plug of yeast in the neck and the bidule nicely settled, take the disgorging key and as you raise the bottle, simultaneously remove the plugged yeast. The key to doing this successfully is to watch the large bubble that is in the bottle and as you start to raise the bottle up to near the horizontal it is possible to see this bubble move. As it does, it is time to open with the disgorging key.

An alternative method is to disgorge into a bucket of water. The water prevents any wine wastage and the wine stops any ingress of water. Whatever process you go for will most likely require plenty of practice to get right and to hone your skill.

Neck freezer used to freeze the yeast post-riddling.

DOSAGE AND TOP-UP

Dosage and top-up provide the last chance to have a positive impact on the wine. Dosage is adding sweetness to balance the acids that are in the wine and, as a rule of thumb, the amount of sugar required is in direct relation to the quantity per litre of acid in the finished wine. As an example, 10g/l TA wines tend to require around 10g/l of sugar to balance the acid – of course, this is only a rough estimation and thorough taste-trialling should be carried out every time, as dosage levels can change with different batches of wine. Longer aged wines will often require less dosage than shorter aged.

Other additions that can be added at this stage are SO_2 at 40ppm, CMC and mannoproteins for enhanced cold stability and mouthfeel respectively. If you were to experience any 'off' aromas or flavours at this stage, then it is also possible to make an addition of copper to rectify this fault.

Disgorging, dosage and top-up unit.

Depending on the size of your operation, a cork and wirer machine could be a great addition to the winery.

Cork and cage on a bottle of sparkling wine.

Dosage is made up as one batch at the start of the day and recipes for this can vary depending on how you are going to deliver the dose. Always ensure, however, that the dosage is the same every time, so that there is consistency in the finished wine. Following the dosage, top-up is then carried out with non-dosaged sparkling wine, so that each bottle contains 750ml of wine.

The wine is then corked and caged. Once caged, let the wine stand vertically before laying down so that the corks do not create a vacuum in bottle. The wine should now be allowed time to blend with the dosage. This process will take a minimum of six weeks to marry the flavours of the dosage and the wine.

PÉT-NAT

Pétillant Naturel, or Pét-Nat, is also known as Méthode Ancestrale and is reputedly the oldest wine-making method in the world. It can be a great way to make

Pét-Nat waiting to be sold or disgorged (depending on your process and the level of carbonation).

wine, as it only requires grapes and some know-how. For a Pét-Nat to be good, the grape quality must be excellent, as there is nothing you can do to change the grapes in the making stage. The wine effectively makes itself and therefore you need sugars and acids in the perfect zones, as you cannot put in any additions.

Finished bottles of Pét-Nat; no additions, no disgorge.

This is one of the main reasons why Pét-Nat has caught the imagination of the general public, as there are no additions. No SO_2, no added sugar, no nutrients – just grape juice that has fermented with indigenous yeasts to put the wines through an alcoholic fermentation.

Before the end of fermentation, the wine is bottled using sparkling wine bottles and is crown-capped. The end of the primary fermentation then takes place within the bottle and as the CO_2 cannot escape, it enters into the wine and creates a naturally sparkling wine.

For your Pét-Nat to be successful, you must ensure that everything the grapes, juice and wine come into contact with is spotlessly clean and sterile. Any bacteria could cause your wines to fail at some stage in their life cycle – or at least cause 'off' flavours.

Obviously with this method nothing is filtered, so be aware that a huge amount of sediment is going to be created. How you handle this sediment is down to you as the maker, but with sediment comes nucleation points, it will cause your wine to gush when it hits oxygen. So, if you are planning to make a Pét-Nat be aware of the amount of CO_2 that you are aiming for in the finished wine. If you aim for Champagne

Foot-pressed and cold-macerated Pét-Nat before indigenous yeast takes over the fermentation.

levels (5–6 bar), you should expect your wine to be very lively and it will definitely require disgorging. If you are aiming for lower levels of CO_2 (2–4 bar), you can still expect gushing and should definitely state on the label that the wine will require chilling and to be stored upright and decanted (similar to a bottle-conditioned ale).

One of the great things about the process is that it means you can start to sell your product almost immediately after the primary fermentation has stopped, which is a huge benefit in comparison to the longer ageing process required to make quality secondary fermented sparkling wines. The wines also go through a stage similar to Beaujolais Nouveau, as the primary fermentation ends in bottle and with the absence of oxygen. It starts to take on almost bubble-gum like flavours that are really unusual and entirely natural.

CHAPTER 9

WINE FAULTS

H_2S

Hydrogen sulphide (H_2S) has an unmistakable aroma of rotten eggs. It is probably the most common wine fault and occurs in the main in cool climates during the primary fermentation stage. One of the reasons it occurs is a lack of nitrogen in the grapes that can be caused due to unripe grapes, low organic matter in the soils, or from very dry growing conditions.

Nitrogen can be measured prior to fermentation and will give the wine maker an indication of whether there is enough nitrogen in the fruit to have a problem-free fermentation. What is being measured is the *yeast assimilable nitrogen* (YAN). For a good, clean fermentation, the YAN figures need to be in the region of 250mg/l.

Hydrogen sulphide can also occur if you have sprayed sulphur on the vines and if there is still some residue on the grape skins when the fermentation process begins. This can make red wine more susceptible than white wines, as the sulphur is on the macerating skins that are in contact with the juice during the fermentation stage. The other main reason is that if you are fermenting in barrels that have been treated with sulphur candles and some of the sulphur is still in barrel, this may cause H_2S to form.

If H_2S is caught early during the fermentation, it is easily corrected with an addition of nutrient such as diammonium phosphate (DAP). If caught late, you need to rack the wine in the first instance, as the H_2S will be even more powerful in the lees and the lees will impart those aromas and flavours further if kept with the wine. By racking the wine, this also introduces oxygen that can cause the H_2S to 'blow off'. A good way of knowing if it is going to work is by taking a small quantity in a wine glass and swirling it vigorously. If the aroma goes, there is a high probability that racking may be enough to sort out your problem.

If not, however, you will have to consider a copper addition. Copper historically was used for taps in wineries for this purpose, so that H_2S would be nullified. If you are going to add any copper, it is important to trial the quantities and use the smallest possible amount. This can be done by adding a known quantity of copper to a solution; with this copper solution you can then trial microdoses of copper 0.1g at a time to 100ml of wine. Once the H_2S clears up in the trial, multiply the dose by the total amount of liquid. Once the H_2S problem has been solved, again rack off the wine after the copper addition.

If you are working with small quantities of wine and have H_2S, simply adding copper coins into the tank will remove the aroma. Again, this can be trialled on a micro-level before adding – it also cleans up the coins at the same time!

ETHYL ACETATE

Ethyl acetate has the aroma of pear at best and nail-varnish remover at worst. Ethyl acetate at low levels

OPPOSITE: **Stirring the lees.**

can contribute to positive aromas in wine, but at high levels it is unpleasant. It can be caused by indigenous yeasts that are not suited for the fermentation, or the combination of acetic acid and oxygen. If wines are left with excess space in the wine tanks, these aromas and flavours can also develop. If you do suspect that you have ethyl acetate, do not try to solve this by adding MLF culture as this will make the problem worse. Unfortunately, there is no practicable way to solve this problem if it should occur.

VOLATILE ACIDITY

Volatile acidity (VA) is associated with the production of vinegar aromas and tastes. Small quantities of VA are produced with every fermentation, often at very low levels, and can lead to wine improvements; however, at higher levels VA will render the wine undrinkable. The problem of VA often occurs if wine-making conditions are not clean, or if wines are introduced to too much oxygen during the wine-making process.

CO_2

Sometimes wines can appear to have an unintended 'prickle' sensation in the mouth, which may be due to an incomplete primary fermentation of MLF that did not entirely finish before bottling. If you are tasting this CO_2 in bottle, it is clearly too late to rectify; however, it may be possible to decant the problem away (or you may decide that you quite like the unusual sensation!).

If you are trying a wine with CO_2 in the tank prior to bottling, it may be possible to rack the wine until the problem no longer exists, or to filter out the offending sugar/bacteria. If you do go down the racking route, be sure to use inert gas in the receiving tanks that the wine is being transferred into, to keep oxygen pick-up to a minimum.

LIGHT STRIKE

Light strike is a very real issue that will ruin your wine, making it taste of cabbages and even onion. It occurs in the wine-storage stage as light passes through the bottles. Ultraviolet (UV) light penetrates the bottle and wine and spoils it. This is the main reason that most beer bottles are produced in brown bottles and most sparkling wine bottles are produced in dark green bottles, as light cannot so easily penetrate bottles of those colours. It should be a consideration in the production of rosé wines, as although the consumer loves to see the pinks of a rosé, the clear glass is a major contributor to light strike.

Storage of your wine is a factor that must be thought through, as light in a warehouse environment can ruin the wine as much as sunlight, so if you have many bottles of wine in storage they should be wrapped in black shrinkwrap at all times, or kept in darkened areas of the winery.

VEGETAL

Vegetal aromas and tastes can occur for a host of reasons and in a cool climate it is often because the fruit used was not totally ripe. If the fruit had yet to reach full maturity and you made wine in a method that did not take this into account, you should expect the wine to taste green. If your fruit is not perfect, consider the following approaches:

- Whole-bunch press, rather than crush and destem – this preserves the grape integrity and will prevent some of the greener flavours from being present in the juice and wine, as there will not be as many phenolic flavours in the juice.
- Ensure that you carefully rack your juice before commencing primary fermentation – so much flavour is stored in the gross lees and any unpleasant ones will be there and magnified if left on the lees during fermentation.
- Choose a yeast strain that will not promote green flavours in the wine.
- Ferment at a cooler temperature to promote fruit flavours as much as possible.
- When fermentation finishes, rack your wine as soon as possible.

MOUSINESS/BRETTANOMYCES

'Mousiness' is not a pleasant aroma; it is somewhat similar to the aroma of a pet shop and the taste can be akin to that of wet wood or leather. It often occurs when no SO_2 has been used in the wine-making process. It is linked with Brettanomyces and lactic-acid bacteria, although there is still a lot that is not known about why it occurs and the threshold at which it becomes perceptible. Good SO_2 procedures in the winery will stop this unwanted flavour in the wines.

STUCK FERMENTATION

If a stuck or sluggish fermentation occurs, it normally does so for a good reason, which can be due to:

- high levels of SO_2
- high sugar content
- alcohol too high
- very cold wine
- low nutrient levels.

To deal with these problems, you can carry out the following actions.

High Levels of SO_2

First, you should rack the juice. Racking will decrease the free SO_2, which may be enough to bring the juice into a range where it can start fermentation. If necessary, retry this process a number of times. If you fail to reduce the free levels enough by racking, consider using hydrogen peroxide to solve the problem. However, hydrogen peroxide can have a negative effect on the wine, so do ensure that any additions are carried out with the absolute minimum quantity. To reduce free SO_2 by 10mg/l, 50g/hl of wine using a 1 per cent hydrogen-peroxide solution can be used. Once you have reduced the SO_2 levels to around 20ppm free, you should try to recommence the primary fermentation.

High Sugar Content

A high sugar content can inhibit yeast activity. The approach to use is to build up the yeast culture by adding it a batch at a time, ensuring that the yeast is happy before adding it to the main batch. Follow the mother-culture build-up procedure in Chapter 8. This process allows the yeast to become acclimatized to the high levels of sugar and prevents any shock that the yeast may develop. It is also recommended to use a yeast suited for traditional-method sparkling wines – these are readily available. During the process, it is wise also to have a good yeast nutrient regime that will aid the yeast during the fermentation.

High Alcohol Content

High alcohol content, like high sugar, can inhibit yeast. Some yeasts are not designed to ferment over a certain ABV, so if you have chaptalized, recheck your additions as you may have added too much sugar. Another common reason for a stuck fermentation is if you are using indigenous yeast. When using indigenous yeasts, it is unknown how they are going to perform and it is likely that they will not have the ability to ferment higher than 8 per cent ABV. If you do get a stoppage, it is wise to pick a strong fermenting yeast that is designed to ferment high ABV wines. Again, applying the process of building up the culture until it is fermenting vigorously is the best way to ensure that you have no issues with the fermentation.

Very Cold Wine

It is recommended to warm up the liquid to as near to 20°C as possible; try pumping over or agitation as the first option. If this fails to restart the fermentation (give it four days), then restart the entire process and try to keep the liquid warm. This can be a big problem, especially if secondary fermentation in sparkling wine is being attempted in winter months when the weather is colder. Do not attempt the secondary fermentation in bottle in winter unless you have a warm environment in which to put the bottles and the wine.

Low Nutrient Levels

If the fermentation fails to complete or is sluggish, it may also be because of low nutrients. If this is the case, bring the nutrients back into the required range. This will normally be in the range of 25–40g/hl with either DAP or organic nutrient. Once in the correct range, pump over; if this fails to start the fermentation, start the yeast protocol again as described in Chapter 8.

PROJECT

CHAPTER 10

TASTE

Scoring wines at a WineGB trade tasting.

When taking groups of people on wine-tasting experiences and tours, I will open the first bottle of wine, pour the wine and then ask the group what they thought. Now, if this group of people are not seasoned wine professionals, the response is often a shrug with a bit of minor embarrassment attached, with members of the group often saying that they are not sure what they can taste. This is interesting – as tasting is something that people do every day – but it is also an understandable response. How to 'taste' wine is something still shrouded in mystery for many – and it shouldn't be! Tasting is a great experience and

OPPOSITE: Giving the wine a good swirl releases more of the aroma compounds.

Appearance and aroma are key parameters when trying wines.

something that is the culmination of all the effort that's gone into making your product. It is far removed from just consuming and in this chapter we will look at how to appreciate what is in the bottle or glass.

Wine tasting is of course subjective. If you like the wine then great, but to look deeper into the tasting element, you want to find out *why* you like the wine. Once you know why you like the wine then you can apply this process again and again and build up a personal preference. Studies show that whether or not you like something will be dictated by your upbringing, culture, education, day to day experiences and life – we are all different.

WINE TASTING

Let's disregard price tags or wine brands here. For the purpose of this section on wine tasting, we're approaching it as a non-faulty wine, poured into a glass, and what to look for and think about as you taste it. The process broadly follows the excellent tasting procedures of the Wine and Spirits Education Trust (WSET).[9]

Wine-tasting events are fun and educational – as you are guided through a range of wines and make friends at the same time.

Balance

Put simply, balance refers to all of the factors that make up the structure of a wine and whether or not these factors are in equilibrium with each other. Most wine makers will be trying to produce a balanced wine and this is the sign of solid wine making; achieving that stability between acidity and perceived sweetness. The other factors that go into the balance of the wines are generally within the inherent qualities of the fruit and as such this is why the greatest wines will always come from the best vineyards and the best plots.

Appearance

When you have been poured your glass of wine, the very first thing to hit you is how it looks. Tilt the glass to a 45-degree angle, which will increase both the light in the glass and the depth of wine to be judged. Look for the clarity, intensity and colour of the wine.[10]

Clarity

If the wine is not clear, it would be pertinent to know why. Is it unfiltered, which is a style of wine making that is becoming increasingly popular, with the rise of the natural wine movement? Or is it completely clear of any sediment? If yes, it doesn't mean that it is filtered; it could have just been well racked. However, most commercially produced wines will be filtered.

Colour

Intensity of colour is as equally applicable to white, red or rosé wines. Is the colour intensity bright, vibrant and one colour throughout? If yes, it is a good indication that the wine is young. If it is not one colour throughout, it is more likely that the wine is aged, or that it has been produced in oak barrels.

When tasting rosé wine, remember that if the colour is dark or light it is not reflective necessarily on the

Wine being poured at one of Renishaw Hall's Vineyard tour and tastes.

quality of a wine, but is an indication of *how* the grape has either been pressed, or if there was any skin contact time. With some varietals, because the skins of the grape are naturally thicker, it can be quite difficult to press in a way that results in a light colour extraction.

With red wines, it would be a reasonable theory that the brighter a wine, the younger it is, whereas the more tawny it is in shade, the older it is (or, at worst, the most oxidized!).

In essence, when it comes to the colour of a wine, respect the varietal and try not to shoehorn the wine into being something it is not, or a colour you perceive to be 'better' or more appealing. It is always preferable to be open-minded regarding what a wine looks like and wait for the taste before making a judgment.

Viscosity

Viscosity comes up much more in wine tasting. There is another potential misconception here, linking the presence of viscosity as a sure indicator of quality, or, put reversely, if you don't witness any viscosity in a wine it means it's not going to be of good quality. If a wine is viscous, this is a result of either sugar or alcohol, so a wine with 'good legs' does not mean it is necessarily higher quality; instead that it has more sugar (or alcohol) content.

CO_2/Presence of Bubbles

If you are drinking wine containing CO_2, it is important to form an educated opinion on how the bubbles got in the bottle. Traditional-method sparkling wine generally contains greater pressure than tank-fermented methods, so this type of wine would tend to have more bubbles. Force-carbonated wine behaves very differently to bottle- or tank-fermented wine, in that the bubble tends to die out faster, therefore it presents a frothier wine but the bubbles don't last as long. Tank-/Charmat-fermented wines sit in the middle and tend to have less CO_2 than traditional method.

Aroma

Hold your glass, give it a swirl and gently take in the aroma. Wine aroma can be so varied and is one of the great pleasures of wine appreciation. A good approach is to decipher the aromas by trying to understand what they are, working 'big' to 'small'. For example, if you are getting fruit as a primary aroma, you can then split it down into what *type* of fruit you can smell. Is it red, citrus, tropical, stone, tree, dried, black fruits?

And from there, you can then narrow down the aroma again into the actual fruit itself. Take a Chardonnay as an example; you might smell citrus and tree fruit. You then need to think: what type of

Making notes and keeping a journal is a great way to get better at wine tasting.

citrus and tree fruit is this? This could then lead you to lime, pear or apple, for example. You could then decode this even further and ask what variety of apple – green/red/ripe/cooked and the same for the other fruits.

Moving away from fruits, if a particular wine has a creamy, lactic aroma and texture on top, then it would be fair to assume that the wine has been through MLF. If you were to pick up even the faintest aroma of vanilla, you could assume the use of oak as well.

This can be replicated for herbaceous and green flavours, nutty, caramel, wood, earth, chemical, pungent, oxidized, floral/flowers and spicy – now dissect these into subsections. Does it smell youthful or old, is it past its best, or is it closed? 'Closed' is a term that means the fruit aromas are in the wine, but just waiting to come out, as the wine develops with time. Decanting a wine can also help to improve the aroma in the short term.

It is also important to think about the condition of the wine. Does it smell clean; is there anything extra that you find unusual? If it is not clean or unusual, can you describe the aroma?

The purpose of the above is to really get under the skin of what you are tasting, to appreciate a wine's style and what the maker was trying to achieve in the process.

FAULTY WINES

Possible faults include cork taint, *reduction*, oxidation, volatile acidity, Brettanomyces and UV damage. These faults can be picked up easily through smelling a wine. The table summarizes some of the key aromas of faulty wine.[11]

Wine Faults

So, returning to those groups who at the start of a tasting session look at me blankly when asked what they can taste; by the end of the session and by knowing that the aromas are there and that most exist in a fruit bowl, fridge or cupboard, this really helps people to understand what they can find within the wine, driving their enthusiasm for the tasting.

Fault	Taste/aroma
Cork taint	Wet cardboard, wet dog, musty cellar
Reduction	Garlic, cabbage, eggs, burnt match, sulphur
Oxidation	Bruised fruit/apples, lack of aroma
Volatile acidity	Vinegar, nail-polish remover
Brettanomyces	Pet shop, mousiness, bandage, sweaty saddle, barnyard, earthy rustic
UV damage	Cabbage

PALATE

Now to the best part – tasting the wine. As you take the wine into your mouth, try and move it around as much as possible and at the same time bring in some oxygen to release as many of the flavours as possible.

What you smell and what you taste are linked, so from the aroma hopefully you are building up a decent picture of the wine as you move on to tasting it. It is mostly the case that what you can smell, you can taste in the drink. Breaking it down into the following taste sections can help to decipher what you get from the wine as you taste it:

Sweetness How sweet is the wine and how did this sweetness get there? If it is a dessert or fortified wine, the sweetness would most likely be down to the production methods of stopping fermentation halfway through. If it is not this style of wine, it's likely that these sugars have been added as opposed to naturally occurring. The right balance of sweetness is one of the most important elements to get right as a producer, understanding who will be buying the wine and what level of sugar will be most appealing.

Acidity If a wine makes you salivate, it has good levels of acid; if it has acidity that feels uncomfortable in your mouth, it has too much acid (for you).

Tannin It is easy to think of this as astringency. If a wine dries and puckers your mouth, it has high levels of tannin – think of a strong cup of tea. Many of the great wines start with high tannin, so this parameter will soften with time, hence the importance of letting wines age.

Alcohol This can often be felt as a burn or heat in the taste. If it is really hot and is burning, there is too much alcohol present. Again, this is about balance – the balance between flavours and the alcohol, so that the sensation of drinking the wine is a pleasurable one.

Body One of the problems in a cool-climate environment is often that the wines lack body and can taste 'thin'. Generally, it takes an exceptional year for cool-climate wines to have real depth. If a wine has body, it will have greater mouthfeel; wines that go through MLF often display more body than wines that do not.

Flavour characteristics This is where we go back to the aroma/taste and think about the flavours that are in the wine.

Length Length could be described as the time for which you can taste the flavour of the wine in your mouth – the longer the flavour, the longer the finish.

Complexity A wine can be described as complex if it has a multitude of flavours and textures. The fewer flavours, the less complex the wine. However, that is not to say that a wine with a single flavour is bad or indifferent, just simple – and there can be excellence in simplicity.

Carbonation If a wine is sparkling, how do you rate it? Small bubbles, big bubbles, aggressive, soft …? Once you have visually assessed, taken in the aroma and tasted the wine, now is the time to form some opinions about whether or not you like the wine. Consider if the wine will get better with time. If the wine is tannic or acidic, will it soften with time? If the wine is lifeless and without structure, it is unlikely that the wine is going to improve or get any better.

TASTING FROM TANK OR BARREL

Directly following fermentation, you will want to see what your wine tastes like at this stage. Just remember, that the wine directly after fermentation will not resemble the finished wine, so do not be too disappointed if the initial taste is not exactly what you were expecting. The wine will most likely taste quite acidic and not very fruit-driven, as the juice whilst still on lees will be closed in flavour in comparison to what it will eventually become.

You will experience the flavour change as the wine goes through each process. It may become fruitier or more expressive in style and it is important to remember that every time you handle the wine it can potentially have long-term negative effects because movement can cause oxidization. Ensure that you use inert gas to flush out tanks and hoses if moving wine. If you have headspace in any of your wine tanks, fill the space with inert gas.

Do not make any blending decisions until you have allowed the wine time to develop and also to stabilize. Bottle shock – a temporary condition where the wine's flavours appear to have significantly changed – is a real thing and signifies the huge chemical changes occurring as the liquid turns from grape juice through to wine. It should not be a surprise that the wine needs time to adjust. A good idea is to keep tasting notes of all the wines prior to getting them into bottle. This will speed up your decision-making process about what you might need to do with the wine, as well as being able to appreciate its evolution.

Tasting wines from tank or barrel and putting together blends is a process that takes years of experience and practice to get right. A back catalogue of wines allows you to understand how your wine is going to develop – for example, when putting together sparkling wines, you would be looking for and expecting a much higher level of acidity than for still wines. Cool-climate wines, also higher in acidity, tend to come into their own after four to five years, so if you can mature your wines in bottle, your customers will really benefit as the wine ages.

TASTING NOTES

We have covered the tasting procedure; your notes when tasting a wine and your own wine could include the following categories:

- type of wine
- when you tasted it
- what stage it was in (barrel/tank/bottle)

- appearance
- aroma
- taste.

OPINION/CONCLUSION

It can be useful (and a bit of fun!) to score the wines. The system is down to you, but something along the lines of five points for appearance, ten points for aroma and ten points for taste will provide a quick reference as to whether you enjoyed a particular wine and how it rates in comparison to the other wines you have tasted.

As you get more skilled at what you are understanding from a wine's aroma, appearance and taste, you will begin to see that there is so much more to take from the wine than simply an enjoyable drink – not least about *how* it was made and even *why* it was made in such a way.

A guided wine tasting at Astley Vineyard.

SEGUIN MOREAU
ENGLISH WINE
PROJECT
R 2021
M

CHAPTER 11

THE BUSINESS OF MAKING WINE

Note: All figures in this section are approximate and reflect costings up to December 2020.

Many people start a wine-making business because of their love of wine, and quite right too! But if it is a wine business and not a wine hobby, it is crucial to know the margins from the production of wine and how much you need to produce to have a business that can support you. After all, success is selling what you produce and with the most profitable outcome. Here are some of the considerations that should be made when starting your business, to inform the best way to proceed.

Renishaw Hall sparkling wine.

OPPOSITE: Oak barrels.

COSTS

Land prices: £10,000 per acre At the time of writing, land prices tend to be around £10,000 per acre on average almost universally across the UK. Obviously, if you are buying huge swathes of land this price decreases, but £10,000 is your ballpark figure.

Vines, wires, posts: £10,000–£15,000 per acre As we know, there are a number of different ways to plant a vineyard. Based on hand-planting a 5-acre vineyard, it is sensible to work off anywhere between £10,000 and £15,000 per acre to plant and install the vineyard. This includes pre-planting operations such as ploughing, power harrowing, vines, vine guards, vine clips, wires and posts. However, this cost does not include extras such as deer fencing, bird netting or anything unusual.

Equipment: £10,000–£20,000 If you are planting anything over a 2-acre vineyard, some machinery will definitely be required. This means tractor, ride-on mower or quad; this equipment will be used to tow a sprayer or pull a mower at the minimum. If budget is no issue, then one could invest in under-vine cultivation machinery, a hedge cutter, a leaf stripper and a whole host of gadgets and devices. Starting figure for this could be £10,000 if shopping around and buying decent second-hand.

As already mentioned, it is possible to do many vineyard tasks for not very much money if you are prepared to carry a knapsack sprayer. This is tough work, carrying a 20kg sprayer up and down the vines, and I would not recommend it unless you are physically fit. However, if you can do it, then do so – as you will only need to invest in a decent mower after that.

Sprays: £500 per annum per acre Expect to pay in the region of £500 per year per acre for spraying. This includes all sprays, both under-vine and on the vine, and fertilizers. You will need to do this for the life cycle of the vine. This also needs to be carried out in the years building up to your first harvest or vintage, which is three years as a minimum, or an average of four years depending on weather conditions.

Labour costs: £2,500 per acre There are a couple of options when it comes to labour: either you do everything yourself and do not put a price on labour, except your own time and value; or, you put a price on labour. The current going rate for all tasks in the vineyard to include pruning, bud rubbing, tucking in, leaf stripping and picking would be in the region of £2 per vine over the year. Bear in mind that these labour costs will be accrued before any grapes are actually produced, so you will have to spend £7,500–£10,000 for the three to four years up to your first crop.

Vineyard at Ashling Park, West Sussex.

Volunteers are a great way to include the community in the project; just don't expect them to turn up when the weather is bad!

Estimated per acre cost to get started:

- £10,000 – land
- £10,000–£15,000 – installation
- £10,000–£20,000 – equipment (second-hand/minimal)
- £500 × four years = £2,000 – sprays
- £2,500 × three years = £7,500 – labour costs
- **£39,500–£54,500** = total start-up cost over three years (including land).

It will cost an estimated £39,500–£54,500 to get up to your first harvest – this is your cash requirement. But you do own the land, and all vines, posts, wires and so on, plus a vehicle – so you have purchased assets. If you have been less lucky with your shopping around for machinery, then the figure is going to be a lot more – perhaps in the region of £60,000 to establish your 1-acre vineyard and buy the required equipment.

PRICE PER TONNE

If you are planning to produce fruit to sell, then the details below will give an indication of how this looks.

A 1-acre vineyard will produce anything from 1t an acre up to 5t on an exceptional plot. A good site will average 3.5t per acre per year over a ten-year period; a marginal site will be far more variable and, as such, 2t is a more realistic average tonnage figure.

The current market rate for buying 1t of classic sparkling wine varietals – Chardonnay, Pinot Noir and Pinot Meunier – is around £2,000. If you have planted Bacchus or Ortega, it is around £1,750 and this decreases to around £1,250 for the Germanic varietals like Madeleine Angevine, Seyval Blanc and Reichensteiner.

If you live on a warm site in the south of England, it will be possible to ripen Chardonnay and achieve £2,000 a tonne, therefore £7,000 per year turnover if you were selling your fruit. It costs per year around £3,000 to grow the fruit. So as a fruit seller, the business model looks pretty good. It should be noted that if you were to get involved with a long-term selling contract, the standard figure for selling fruit would decrease to nearer £1,500 per tonne.

If you are converting this fruit into wine, it is important to understand the press fractions and juice extraction; this will tell you how much potential wine you are going to make from the grapes. 1t of grapes destined for still wine is generally around 70 per cent extraction to weight. So a tonne will produce 700l of juice. If you were pressing for a cuvée, this figure is closer to 51 per cent extraction, therefore there is around 10–20 per cent potential extraction not accounted for. This could be used for blending later or to be introduced to still wines, as this juice contains more flavour and therefore may not suit a sparkling wine style.

Working off extraction of 70 per cent with 1t of fruit to show how the business could work:

- You now have 700l of juice. After the first rack you are going to lose approximately 2 per cent before putting the wine through fermentation. Following fermentation, you rack again and lose approximately 3 per cent further in fermentation lees. Post-maturation time, filtration plus stabilization and bottling means you lose a further 5 per cent.
- Now your 700l has yielded 630l of wine. This equates to 840 bottles per tonne; 3.5t means 840 bottles × 3.5t = 2,940 bottles from your 1-acre vineyard at a cost of £3,000 per acre in labour and spraying costs. Therefore, each bottle in vineyard terms cost £1.02 (a good price per bottle). However, if you do not get 3.5t an acre, but actually nearer 2t an acre, the cost per bottle will start to rise rapidly.

CONTRACT WINE-MAKING COSTS

The figures used in this section are average prices, though clearly contract wine-making charges will vary from business to business. There are always a few charges that can take you by surprise – for example, pressing charges, cardboard, labelling and admin – so keep this in mind when you are budgeting.

Pressing charges £300 for the first tonne and £100 per tonne thereafter.

Still wine On average £2.20 a bottle, though this is dependent on quantity and will be worked out based on pressing efficiency, but also on tank space. If the winery is configured for a certain size of tank, that space is going to want to be maximized. If you are producing less than 1,000l, the cost is likely to be more, while over 2,000l it is likely to be less. There will be around a 10 per cent difference in price either way.

To produce still wine from your 3.5t of English-grown grapes it is going to cost £550 in pressing charges and £6,468 in wine-making costs to produce 2,940 bottles of still wine. The total cost is £7,018, therefore £2.39 per bottle.

Selling fruit can be a great way to keep cash flow moving for the wine business.

Sparkling wine £5.00 per bottle is the normal price for a contract-made bottle of sparkling wine. For more or less quantities, expect to pay 5 per cent either way of this price. To produce a bottle of sparkling wine will cost you £550 in pressing charges and £14,700 in wine-making charges, therefore £15,250 or £5.19 per bottle.

It should also be noted that the production of quality sparkling wine means at least an extra year in the bottle, so you will be paying the £15,250 twice before you start selling, an important consideration for your cash flow.

It is worth talking to as many contract wine makers as possible, not to bargain the price down, but to find a team that you are happy with. Medals and awards are of course a useful indicator of the quality of the team, but also pay an interest to the set-up of the winery, the cleanliness and their attitude, who you are going to be dealing with and – ultimately – make sure that you like them.

It is rather harder to quantify the price per bottle when making wine yourself, as once you own the equipment the per-bottle making charge will be in the region of 50–60 per cent of the total production cost of taking it to a contract wine maker. There is also the time implication of making it yourself, plus the cost of buying all the equipment. As can be seen later in this chapter, that cost does not have to be very high for small-scale production.

DUTY

A big cost and something that has to be taken into consideration is duty. Please find below the current duty rates as of February 2019:

- £2.23 for still wine per bottle
- £2.86 for sparkling wine per bottle.

Adding this duty to your bottle prices and you have £4.62 for a bottle of still wine and £8.06 for a bottle of sparkling wine.

Now you can add grape-growing charges at £1.02 and costs are £5.64 for still wine and £9.08 for sparkling. It is worth noting that grape growing at £1.02 a bottle is conservative, but more on the price of fruit/cost of growing it later in the chapter.

LABELS, BOXES AND TRANSPORT

Labels Label prices are worked out on economies of scale and how technical the labels are, with features like gold foil and raised font costing extra. If you are only buying a few hundred labels, the cost could be around £1 per label per bottle for front and back labels. If you are buying a few thousand labels, these costs will decrease to around £0.30p a bottle.

State of the art contract wine-making facilities at Defined Wine in Kent.

Always shop around for labels and speak to other producers to find out who has been good value, but also who has provided a great service. In the end, it is better to pay more for fewer mistakes and if there is a mistake that is the fault of the label company, any reputable company should always offer to rectify the issue with no hassle.

Boxes Boxes can be worked out at £0.10p per bottle for a very basic box (£0.60p per box). To buy branded boxes, you will need to order 1,000+ boxes. If this is prohibitive – as you are not producing enough wines for a company to brand your boxes – consider what your requirements are. If you just need a box to store wine, a single-skinned box will suffice.

If you plan to send your wines in transit it is necessary to investigate the best product for this task and this is where packaging does become expensive. Whatever option you go for, ensure that the wine does get there in one piece and also that the cost is incorporated in the sale price, or the p&p costs.

Transport Moving a pallet of wine is around £50 per pallet. Assuming 600 bottles on a pallet, this figure is £0.08 per bottle.

These extras cited here can therefore add anything from £0.50p to over £1 a bottle. Let's assume for the purposes of calculation that you have done a great job sourcing the best-priced items and so will price labels, boxes and transport costs at £0.50p a bottle.

TOTAL CONTRACT WINE-MAKING COSTS (INCLUDING VINEYARD)

Assuming 3.5t in your own vineyard:

Still wine:

- £1.02 in the vineyard
- £2.39 wine-making charges
- £2.23 duty
- £0.50 labels, boxes and transport
- **£6.14 total per bottle.**

Sparkling wine:

- £1.02 in the vineyard
- £5.19 winemaking sparkling
- £2.86 duty
- £0.50 labels, boxes and transport
- **£9.57 total per bottle.**

There are a lot of costs to consider when setting up a wine business – you need to have passion for the product.

YIELD

A yield of 3.5t is a healthy average and would be very difficult to achieve in cooler parts of the country. Therefore, it is of utmost importance that the grape variety is the most suitable for the part of the country in which it is growing and not a variety chosen because it is your favourite grape. It has to be able to crop and produce ripe fruit. The following shows the difference in price per bottle if we only get 1t and 2t per acre:

- 1t = 840 bottles/£3,000 = £3.57 per bottle
- 2t = 1,680 bottles/£3,000 = £1.78 per bottle.

These figures show that unless there is optimal cropping in the vineyard, the business very quickly can become non-profitable and untenable if you have a series of failed crops or a low-cropping site.

BUYING FRUIT INSTEAD OF GROWING IT

If your vineyard has a bad year, or you just want to expand your operation without buying or leasing more land and planting vines, an option is buying in fruit to make wine. The economics of this are interesting, given the current market rate for different varieties as mentioned earlier in the chapter.

If you have a high-cropping site, it makes sense to grow your own fruit, but if you are around the 2t an acre mark it is the better option to buy in fruit – certainly if you can secure it for around £1,500 per tonne. The figures in the table, based on 1t = 840 bottles, will express this clearly.

Relative Costs When Buying in Fruit

Tonnage	Bottles	Cost per tonne	Cost per bottle
1	840	£2,000	£2.38
1	840	£1,800	£2.14
1	840	£1,600	£1.90
1	840	£1,400	£1.67
1	840	£1,200	£1.43
1	840	£1,000	£1.19

The figures in the table also show that the difference between the most expensive and the cheapest fruit equates to £1.19. When one considers that the whole venture rests on fruit it would seem that buying the best fruit is a more sensible option than buying cheaper fruit. This is certainly the case if you are using contract wine-making services. Ultimately it comes down to how much you can sell your wine for and if there is margin.

STILL WINE PRODUCTION COSTS

Let's put these costs into the matrix and see how viable the business is if you are solely a still wine producer.

Relative Costs of Still Wine Production

	Buying fruit	Wine-making charges	Duty	Labels, boxes, transport	Total ex. VAT	Total incl. VAT
£2,000p/t	£2.38	£2.39	£2.23	£0.50	£7.50	£9.00
£1,800p/t	£2.14	£2.39	£2.23	£0.50	£7.26	£8.71
£1,600p/t	£1.90	£2.39	£2.23	£0.50	£7.02	£8.42
£1,400p/t	£1.66	£2.39	£2.23	£0.50	£6.78	£8.14
£1,200p/t	£1.43	£2.39	£2.23	£0.50	£6.54	£7.84
£1,000p/t	£1.19	£2.39	£2.23	£0.50	£6.30	£7.56

The figures in this table are interesting when you consider how much margin a wine merchant will want to make and what price your wine can command. Let's assume that the merchant is after a 33 per cent margin and you are selling your wine at £7.50 ex. VAT; the merchant will be looking to sell the wine for:

- £9.00 total price inc. VAT + 33% (£4.41) = £13.41.

So, although not an expensive wine, this is considerably more than a lot of wines on the shelves. I have put together a table that gives an indicative pricing structure.

Indicative Pricing Structure

Price ex. VAT	Price inc. VAT (20%)	Margin (33%)	Shelf RRP
£7.50	£9.00	£4.41	£13.41
£8.50	£10.20	£5.00	£15.20
£9.50	£11.40	£5.59	£16.99
£10.50	£12.60	£6.17	£18.77

Therefore, unless you are going to be producing wines at very high volume there really is not a huge amount of money to be made selling to trade and certainly not at the entry-level end of the market. However, selling to trade will keep cash flowing in your business, so it should make up a proportion of your sales plan. What is clear is that selling directly yields by far the best returns and should be investigated thoroughly as to how to carry out this function successfully. This could be online sales or directly. One of the best ways of carrying out sales for the small vineyard is to link this activity to some form of tourism offer, where you can add value and impart knowledge and the experience you have gone through to create your wines.

SPARKLING WINE PRODUCTION COSTS

Sparkling wine:

- £1.02 in the vineyard
- £5.19 wine-making sparkling
- £2.86 duty
- £0.50 labels, boxes and transport
- **£10.59 total per bottle.**

There is little margin in selling to supermarkets and wholesalers, unless you are dealing with large volumes. Selling direct, one would hope to achieve around £25+ for a bottle of sparkling and £13+ for a still wine including VAT. If selling to trade, we know that an off-trade mark-up is around 33 per cent, therefore £25–VAT @ 20 per cent = £20; 33 per cent of £20 is £6, so the sale price will be around £14 for sparkling.

For the small wine-production business the advice therefore should be to establish an attractive vineyard and to produce the best fruit possible. Once this has been achieved, the next challenge is to get as many visitors as possible to your vineyard and sell wine and vineyard tours.

The figures also show that the business of sparkling wine is far more favourable than still wine, but the cost of production is much higher and actually what makes the business look unappealing is the amount of time the wine needs in secondary fermentation. This is both a positive and negative aspect, as the wine is also improving whilst on its lees. However, passing on this cost is difficult if the customer does not know or understand that the wine is improving in bottle.

Relative Costs of Sparkling Wine Production

	Buying fruit	Wine-making Charges	Duty	Labels, Boxes, Transport	Total ex. VAT	Total inc. VAT
£2,000p/t	£2.38	£5.19	£2.86	£0.50	£10.93	£13.12
£1,800p/t	£2.14	£5.19	£2.86	£0.50	£10.69	£12.83
£1,600p/t	£1.90	£5.19	£2.86	£0.50	£10.45	£12.54
£1,400p/t	£1.66	£5.19	£2.86	£0.50	£10.21	£12.25
£1,200p/t	£1.43	£5.19	£2.86	£0.50	£9.98	£11.98
£1,000p/t	£1.19	£5.19	£2.86	£0.50	£9.74	£11.69

MAKING YOUR OWN WINE

If putting together a commercial winery that can process around 20t (14,000l), expect to pay around £100,000 for a mixture of new and used equipment. Typical costs are presented below in the table.

If your project is less than 20t and is around 1t, it clearly does not make any sense to invest in £100,000 worth of machinery – so what is the alternative? Your options are to send it off to a contract wine maker or produce it yourself. If you are trained, or at least are willing to make a few mistakes along the way, how much do you need to spend and how much space do you need? First, if you are a site producing around 1t, you can easily make wine in a room the size of a single garage, so if you have a garage, you have a winery. The approximate prices for small-scale wine production are outlined in the table.

If you are producing small quantities of wine, starting your own winery makes more commercial and practical sense – it is more fun as well!

Equipment Costs for a Commercial Winery (20T)

Equipment	Price (ex. VAT)	Remarks
Grape press	£15,000	second-hand
Crush/destemmer	£3,000	second-hand
Pump	£1,000	new
Tanks (14,000l of tank)	£22,000	double-jacketed
Tank rouser	£1,000	new
Hose (3 × 5m)	£360	£24 per metre
Earth filter	£4,000	second-hand
Cartridge filter	£1,500	new
Chilling unit	£5,000	second-hand
Compressor	£300	new
Six-head filler	£1,300	new

Equipment	Price (ex. VAT)	Remarks
Corker/wirer	£9,000	new – you could save money with a manual device, but for nearly 20,000 bottles I would prefer automatic kit
Neck freezer	£3,850	new
Pupitre × 5	£1,000	new
Jet wash	£200	new
Steamer	£3,000	new
Storage/stillages × 20	£2,000	new
Total	**£73,510**	**ex. VAT**

Costs for Small-Scale Wine Production

Equipment	Price (ex. VAT)	Remarks
Grape press	£1,500	basket press/hydropress
Crush/destemmer	£0	not required, can be done by hand or whole-bunch press the fruit
Pump	£300	small pump
Tanks	£1,000	Stainless-steel tank single skin for £1 a litre or IBC or plastic tanks
Hose (2 × 5m)	£40	
Earth filter	£0	no filter required – racking only
Cartridge filter	£0	not required
Chilling unit	£0	not required – cold-stabilize outside or use CMC
Compressor	£150	new
Six-head filler	£1,300	new
Corker/wirer	£300	manual kit
Neck freezer	£	
Pupitre × 5	£0	make your own with old pallets
Jet wash	£200	new
Total	**£4,790**	**ex. VAT**

For a £5,000 investment, it is therefore possible to produce wines oneself and it is going to be so much more rewarding than simply sending your fruit off to a contract wine maker. There is also the option to employ wine-making consultants to help you in the first few years, to show you how to make no-faults wine. Once you have the basic knowledge, you can then experiment with different processes and find your own way and style of making.

DIVERSIFY

To add value to the customer and to take on and win against the big producer you simply have to have a tourism element to your business. This could be organized vineyard tours, yoga in the vineyard, winery tours or wine tastings. The consumer wants to have a good time and they want to have an experience they will remember. If you can combine this in your space and sell wine at the same time, you will go a long way towards winning important local support and also having a good time in the process. Typical prices for a vineyard tour range from £10 to £20 per person, depending on the offer. These tours offer one to two hours of guiding people through the process from grape growing to wine making and are a lot more fun than attending your average food fair.

Vineyard tours are a great way to diversify and welcome people to the vineyard.

CHAPTER 12

TERROIR AND CONCLUSIONS

Sunset at the Bolney Estate in West Sussex.

To take the vine, nurture it, watch it grow and – eventually – bear fruit, is a hugely rewarding experience. It does not require a huge space or budget. On a modest patch of land – the sort of space where you might grow roses – why not grow vines instead? As long as there's the sunlight and enough drainage, you can make it work and grow enough grapes to produce wine; in other words, 'grow your own wine'.

OPPOSITE: **A hugely rewarding activity – you just need passion and perseverance to get started.**

Terroir can be described as 'somewhereness' – Astley Park Vineyard.

Like any gardener knows, growing vines and maintaining a vineyard – from a few rows long to several hectares large – is not a seasonal job. There is always something to do, even in the depths of winter, when the vines are at their most dormant or in late spring, when you don't know which way to turn for vineyard jobs to do. But with a little perseverance and a lot of passion, you will get there!

If you do not have any land on which to grow grapes, you can of course still make wine, in itself a massively satisfying, as well as skilled, achievement. Why not contact your local vineyard or greengrocer and buy some grapes, then, armed with a few demijohns and the knowledge from this book, make your own wine, following the same principles as a large winery. Once you have gained the passion for and knowledge of wine making, it will help you to appreciate wines from all over the country and the world, and their terroirs.

TERROIR

Terroir is interesting and important, but also intuitive. If one grows grapes on a particular patch of land and somebody else grows the same varietal somewhere else, the fruit will taste different. The differences are as a result of geographical location, production and – not least – the principles and practices behind production.

Terroir can be understood by the term 'somewhereness'. It is the sum of all the parts that go into the production of the fruit. It is everything about the site – be it the slope, topography, trees, water, soil, flora, wildlife, through to more macro aspects such as weather and latitude. Whether or not one's terroir can be 'better' than one somewhere else can be debated and debated; but what can be agreed is that it will be different and it is these differences that we hope to portray to the consumer so that they can appreciate them.

Why is terroir important? Because it is a true reflection of provenance and uniqueness. It should not be possible to create the exact same tastes from a different place, even if it is just a few miles down the road. So, for the grower, producer and the final consumer, this should excite them to produce and taste the wares of the exact place of where a vine grows.

We are fortunate in the UK that we have many different soils in such a relatively small country and that regionally there are massive variations. Vines grown on chalk, gravel, greensands and clay produce vastly different wines that are a direct reflection of the area in which the vines are grown. We want to celebrate these differences – however subtle – so that the consumer can try something different and form their own opinion of what they enjoy. Therefore, seek to do the very best at all times with your fruit and understand what your wines can achieve and realize their potential – it is important.

Local really does matter and fantastic wines can be made anywhere in the UK, but they have to be made with thought, care and attention and it is always better to be thinking long term instead of short with your production methods. This could mean something as simple as understanding that your grapes will be better suited to sparkling wine, or that the red grapes you have grown will make a great rosé, but a less impressive red wine. Hopefully, this book has explained how you need to understand what your grapes can do to get the best out of them, what they are best suited to and how you can handle them in the best possible way, so that you can produce delicious wine that ultimately will be enjoyed by the people who taste it.

Walls surrounding the vines at Renishaw Hall Vineyard.

Busy trade tasting enjoying many bottles of English wine.

Wine is one of the few alcoholic drinks that is a product of terroir and it's true to say that great wines can only be made using great grapes. However, what is not true is to suggest that great wine can only be made from a select few sites in the UK. Wine can be produced across the length and breadth of the UK, but to be a great wine is a more difficult challenge; where patience, attention to detail and understanding of what you are trying to achieve should be understood at all times. Vines live under the same skies, breathe in the same air and express themselves in the fruit that they produce. For native wine makers, it is vital for consumers to go for interesting and local wherever possible, as opposed to something that follows the mainstream.

Llanerch Vineyard near Cardiff hosting its ever-popular vineyard tours.

CLIMATE CHANGE

It is definitely not to be ignored that climate change is having a huge impact on the world of wine, with great wine regions now experiencing weather that consistently delivers big, bold-style wines, not necessarily in keeping with their spiritual ethos. Pinot Noirs from Burgundy that once delivered more ethereal wines are now producing jammy blockbusters that would be more recognized in the hot climes of the south of France.

The same is undoubtedly true of England – and not just the south-east. It is more than possible to ripen the grapes traditionally associated with Champagne here in the UK, on the same soil types as the great region. In the best years it has been known to reach the same levels of phenolic ripeness, the same sugars, acids and even yields of some areas of Champagne.

It looks like these altered weather conditions are here to stay, which could mean year on year improved growing conditions for grape and wine production. Where will it end? Some projections indicate that some areas of the south of England will actually end up being too warm for sparkling wine varietals and will be focused on reds, with sparkling wine production headed further north. If the world of wine started now, would Bordeaux plant Cabernet Sauvignon and Merlot? Burgundy, Pinot Noir and Chardonnay? Champagne – Pinot Noir, Meunier and Chardonnay? All very unlikely. Would the UK plant Pinot Noir and Chardonnay? Yes, it would.

CONCLUSIONS

If you are producing wine on a small scale and have enjoyed the process and want to go bigger, then go for it! However, do so fully understanding the costs, margins and time involved. It can be a stressful business and hugely taxing financially. You are also at the whim of nature when producing fruit and this

Ideal growing conditions for sparkling wines at Little Wold Vineyard, Yorkshire.

means that putting together a business plan can be hit or miss, depending on how much fruit your vineyard can produce in a year. It's probably wisest to say plan for the worst and hope for the best ...! However, grape growing and wine producing is a fantastic pastime, part-time business or full-time venture – and it is great fun. Along the way, you will meet brilliant, like-minded people who are either producing already or want to begin like you.

Wine making is an incredibly rewarding activity that makes you want to keep producing, to do something better than last year, perhaps to do something different, when you not only see the fruits of your labour in grapes, but then get the opportunity to produce wine. And, although scientific, wine making is also artistry, allowing the producer at every point to make a decision that will change the wine for the better (or for the worse). You can be precise in every choice you make in the wine-making process – for example, choosing stainless steel over oak, non-MLF over MLF, controlled ferment temperature over no temperature control, known yeast or indigenous yeast ... the list of things that will alter your wine goes on and on. Look after the grapes at every step of the way and look after the wines both pre-bottle and post-bottle. Whatever you decide to do, it should be with a plan in mind, but with room for flexibility and with care at the forefront of all you do; that way you will get the best results.

What is crucial to the success of wine in our nation is that people buy and support local. If you enjoy wine, visit your local vineyard and get involved, help out at harvest, find out about pruning, take a walk through the vines when the sun is beating down and try the wines. Your support of your local vineyard will mean more than you can imagine. Every bottle sold – whether buying direct from the winery, from a local village fair, or from one of the many brilliant wine specialists and farm shops located across the country – goes towards keeping the UK vineyards and wine production going. If we can build on the culture whereby we do 'grow our own', support our locality and buy our produce from our local villages and towns wherever we can, we can start to reverse the worrying inevitability of a country that's one big, homogenous soulless place.

Late-harvest Rondo being picked at Renishaw Hall Vineyard.

Supporting your local vineyard is so important for the small producer.

I hope you have enjoyed reading this book. Its purpose has been to guide you to grow and produce grapes and make the best wine you can. There are, of course, many different ways to do everything described here and this is one of the joyous elements of the activity; the smallest tweaks to the process can have a big impact. Behind every bit of advice is experience and along the way I have learnt that there really isn't a 'right' way of making wine and as such this book is intended as a direction, a steer, and – like all the most rewarding journeys in life – it is best for you to find your own way with this book at your side.

Thank you for reading.

REFERENCES

[1] www.englishwine.com

[2] www.winegb.co.uk

[3] Skelton, S., *Wine Growing in Great Britain* (Stephen Skelton, 2020).

[4] Steiner, R., *Agriculture Course – The Birth of the Biodynamic Method* (Rudolf Steiner Press, 2004), p.122.

[5] Smart, R. and Robinson, M., *Sunlight Into Wine* (Wine Titles, 1991), p.48.

[6] Smart, R. and Robinson, M., *ibid.*, p.2.

[7] Goode, J., *Wine Science* (Mitchell Beazley, 2014), p.112.

[8] Zoecklein, B., Fugelsang, K., Gump, B. and Nury, F., *Wine Analysis and Production* (CBS Publishers, 1997), pp.173–4.

[9] Fielden, C., *Exploring the World of Wines and Spirits* (Wine and Spirits Education Trust, 2009), p.44.

[10] Jackson, R., *Wine Tasting: A Professional Handbook* (Elsevier, 2009).

[11] Puckette, M. and Hammack, J., *Wine Folly* (Penguin Books, 2018), p.29.

GLOSSARY

Adenosine triphosphate (ATP) Carrying energy within cells, this molecule provides the drive and power in all living things, useful to know when checking sterility.

Autolytic Deriving from a chemical reaction between the wine and lees, imparting characteristics such as aromas of bread, brioche.

Bâtonnage Stirring wine lees in barrel to create extra depth of flavour.

Biodynamic (biological dynamic) Holistic approach that combines the use of cosmic cycles and other ecological organic practices.

Brettanomyces (brett) Unwanted yeast that can develop in unclean wineries and leads to pet-shop aromas and mousiness in wine.

Brix, baume, specific gravity (SG) or Oeschle Systems for the measurement of density and sugars in grape juice prior to fermentation.

Budburst Stage of vine development with the start of the exposure of the first leaves.

Cane One-year-old shoot that has now lignified and can be tied down to create the fruiting arm (cane pruning) or jettisoned.

Chaptalize Adding sugar to increase the potential alcohol of juice prior to fermentation.

Clone Genetically identical vine types.

Co-inoculating Adding yeast and MLF bacteria at the same time so that the bacteria benefits from the increase in temperature caused by the primary fermentation.

Crushing and destemming Wine-making procedure where the grapes are separated from the stalks, used almost all of the time for red wine, most of the time for white wine and occasionally for sparkling wines.

De-acidification To lower acidity through MLF or chemical means.

Diacetyl By-product of a MLF that can produce buttery flavours.

Diammonium phosphate (DAP) Widely used nutrient to promote fault-free fermentations.

Disgorging Removal of the frozen plug of yeast in the sparkling wine-making process.

Dosage Adding sugar to balance the acidity in sparkling wine post-disgorging.

Enzyme Proteins that increase the speed of settling, increase yield when macerating and can increase aromatic profile.

Ethyl acetate Commonly produced in wine; in high amounts can smell strongly of pear-drop sweets or nail-varnish remover.

Fermentation Process of turning sugar into alcohol with the presence of yeast.

Fining Removing proteins in juice or wine and can help with clarity.

Grape must Freshly pressed grapes that contain solids.

Growing degree days Days that exceed 10°C in the growing season – can be a useful indicator as to the suitability of a wine region.

Guyot A system for grapevine trellising.

Guyot-Poussard A system for grapevine trellising that is focused on the sap flow of the vine.

Herbicide Commonly known as weedkiller.

Hydrogen sulphide (H_2S) The aroma of rotten eggs, caused by fermenting juice that is low in nitrogen.

Hydrometer Device used to measure the relative density of juice that will provide a potential alcohol reading.

Inflorescence Stage of grape development prior to cap fall and flowering.

Integrated pest management (IPM) An approach to viticulture that incorporates practices across traditional and organic viticulture.

Intermediate bulk containers (IBC) Used for transporting liquids.

Lees Sediment from wine post-fermentation that drops to the bottom of the tank or barrel.

Light strike UV light penetrating bottles of wine in storage that can lead to cabbage and onion flavours and aromas in wine.

Maceration Used to extract colour, aroma or flavour from fermenting grapes or must.

Malolactic fermentation (MLF) Bacteria converts malic acid (green apple) to lactic acid (dairy) whilst decreasing total acidity.

Mycorrhizal Beneficial fungus in the plant's root system.

Nodes Located on the vine and houses the bud growth system; nodes are encouraged at desired locations on the fruiting arms of the vine.

Organic viticulture No synthetic non-carbon products can be applied in an organic vineyard.

Peracetic acid (PAA) Used to sterilize.

Pétillant Naturel (Pét-Nat) Spontaneous primary fermentation that finishes in bottle to give a naturally sparkling wine.

pH Measure of the acidity in wine. Most English wines will be between 2.9 and 3.5pH. The lower the pH, the more acidic it is.

Phenolic ripeness Ripeness of all parts of the grape and stalk, and not fixated on sugars.

Potential alcohol The level of sugar in a juice that would be converted to alcohol after primary fermentation.

Pulp The grape flesh beneath the skin.

Pump over Pumping over fermenting juice on to the grapes to extract more colour and tannin.

Punch down Punching down fermenting grapes to extract more colour and tannin.

Racking Moving juice or wine from point A to B.

Reduction Too little exposure to oxygen during fermentation can lead to a wine that can become 'eggy'.

Refractometer Device used to measure sugars in the vineyard.

Riddling Process of working the dead yeast cells in sparkling wine into the neck of the bottle using a pupitre or gyro-pallette.

Rootstock The vine is grafted on to a rootstock that has suitable attributes for the vineyard in which it is planted.

Saccharomyces cerevisiae Yeast responsible for the majority of fermentations; also known as brewers' yeast.

Spur pruning Pruning method leaving a permanent fruiting arm on the fruiting wire.

Stability Protein, tartaric (cold) and microbial stability must be obtained before wine is bottled.

Sterility Completely clear of living organisms, achieved with steam or PAA.

Sulphur dioxide (SO_2) Prevents oxidation and spoilage in wine.

Tannin Provides increased texture in wines and is found in the skins and stalks; plus oak fermentation and ageing can increase tannins.

Tartrates Wine crystals visible in wine; can be avoided through cold stability.

Terroir 'Somewhereness' – the sum of all parts of a place from where a wine is created.

Tirage Yeast and sugar solution that goes into the base wine to create the conditions for a secondary fermentation.

Total acidity The amount of acid in a wine, normally expressed as grams per litre (g/l).

Traditional method Secondary fermentation in bottle.

Veraison Grapes changing colour and ripening in the vineyard.

Volatile acidity Most notable is acetic acid; too much and the wine can taste of vinegar.

Yeast assimilable nitrogen (YAN) Analysis of YAN at the grape stage gives an indication of whether or not further nitrogen additions are required throughout the fermentation.

APPENDICES

APPENDIX I – WINE-MAKING LOG

DATE:		VINEYARD:	VARIETAL:			VINTAGE:	QUANTITY (T/KG):			QUANTITY AFTER PRESS (L):
INITIAL READINGS:		OESCHLE:	TA:				pH:			
DATE	WINERY PROCEDURE	ADDITION	QUANTITY ADDITION	TEMP (°C)	OESCHLE	POTENTIAL ALCOHOL	TA (g/l)	pH	FREE SO_2	REMARKS/ COMMENTS

APPENDIX II – WHITE WINE PRODUCTION TABLE

Serial	Winery Procedure	Addition	Typical Quantities	Remarks
	DAY 1			
1	Grapes arrive			log in the grape and weigh, note any imperfections in the fruit
2	Crush/destem	SO_2	40ppm	crush and destem as required – you may choose to whole bunch press. If producing rosé wine then you may need to press harder or change the settings at the crush – varietal dependent
3	Enzyme addition	add enzyme	1–2g/hl	maceration enzyme
4	Take sugar and acid readings and measure quantities			Oeschle and TA
5	Prepare bentonite		25g/hl	mix into a slurry in 10× its weight in water and settle for 24 hours
6	Allow to settle for 24 hours			to remove gross lees
	DAY 2			
7	If very high acid consider chemical de-acidification	potassium bicarbonate	1g/l	1g/l will reduce acidity by 1%
8	Rack juice			
9	Note exact quantity of juice			
10	Add bentonite	bentonite	25g/hl	
11	Take sugar and acid readings again	add sugar as required		17g/l will lead to 1% increase in ABV – aim for 11.5% ABV white wine and 10.5% ABV sparkling base wine
12	Add protecting nutrient	organic nutrient desirable	40g/hl	
13	Add yeast	yeast	25g/hl	add a suitable yeast for your varietal
	DAY 3			
14	Add MLF bacteria if desired	MLF bacteria	cx instructions	ensure that your bacteria is designed for co-inoculation
	1–4 weeks			
15	Add nutrient	⅓ and ⅔ through fermentation	50g/hl	can be DAP or organic

16	Monitor fermentation			use hydrometer and check for off aromas – add DAP if any bad smells
17	Add MLF bacteria if desired	MLF bacteria	cx instructions	follow protocol if desired
18	Fermentation completion	SO_2 addition	40ppm	if no MLF add SO_2
19	Enzyme addition	add enzyme	1–2g/hl	aroma enzyme
20	Rack wine			this is down to you as a wine maker and is lees-dependent: 6–8 weeks if clean lees; if there are any signs of H_2S during fermentation, then rack
	Post-fermentation			
21	Check SO_2	SO_2 addition	40ppm	
22	Check protein stability			if not protein-stable, carry out fining trials
23	Cold stabilize	CMC if no cooling jackets	100ml/hl	follow instruction
24	Once protein and cold-stable, move to bottling stage			
25	Filter	earth or pad filter		
26	Final SO_2 checks		aim for 40ppm	no more than 40ppm free SO_2
27	Sterile filter and bottle			ensure sterility of all hoses and filling heads – if sterile bottling, ensure 0.45μ

APPENDIX III – SPARKLING WINE PRODUCTION TABLE

Serial	Winery Procedure	Addition	Typical Quantities	Remarks
	DAY 1			
1	Grapes arrive			log in the grape and weigh, note any imperfections in the fruit
2	Whole-bunch press	SO_2	40ppm	you may choose to crush and destem as opposed to whole-bunch press
3	Take sugar and acid readings and measure quantities			Oeschle and TA
4	Prepare bentonite		25g/hl	mix into a slurry in 10× its weight in water and settle for 24 hours

5	Allow to settle 24 hours			to remove gross lees – this will be light as you have given the grapes a light press
6	**DAY 2**			
7	If very high acid, consider chemical de-acidification	potassium bicarbonate	1g/l	1g/l will reduce acidity by 1%
8	Rack juice			
9	Note exact quantity of juice			
10	Add bentonite	bentonite	25g/hl	
11	Take sugar and acid readings again	add sugar as required		17g/l will lead to 1% increase in ABV – aim for 10–10.5% ABV sparkling base wine
12	Add protecting nutrient	organic nutrient desirable	40g/hl	
13	Add yeast	yeast	25g/hl	add a suitable yeast for sparkling wine
	DAY 3			
14	Add MLF bacteria if desired	MLF bacteria	cx instructions	ensure that your bacteria is designed for co-inoculation (highly recommended in cool-climate wine making)
	1–4 weeks			
15	Add nutrient	⅓ and ⅔ through fermentation	50g/hl	can be DAP or organic
16	Monitor fermentation			use hydrometer and check for 'off' aromas – add DAP if any bad smells
17	Add MLF bacteria if desired	MLF bacteria	cx instructions	follow protocol if desired
	Fermentation completion	SO_2 addition	40ppm	if no MLF add SO_2
18	Enzyme addition	Add enzyme	1–2g/hl	aroma enzyme (if desired) after fermentation
19	Rack wine			this is down to you as a wine maker and lees dependent; 2–4 weeks for sparkling base wine is a recommended time frame

	Post-fermentation and MLF			
20	Check SO_2	SO_2 addition	40ppm	
21	Check protein stability			if not protein stable carry out fining trials
22	Cold stabilize	CMC if no cooling jackets	100ml/hl	follow instruction
	Once protein- and cold-stable move to bottling stage			
23	Filter	earth or pad filter		it may be possible to rack successfully instead of filtering
	Build mother culture (Day 1)			**Aim for 20ppm SO_2 free at the start of the process**
24	Yeast and water			maintain at 20°C – after 20 minutes stir gently
25	**20 minutes later**			
26	Yeast, nutrient and water mix is added to base wine and liquer mix	nutrient required		50:50 sugar to liquer ratio. Aim for 1.065 SG – maintain the temperature of the liquid at 20°C. Mix and aerate daily. Mother culture will be approximately 4–5% of the total quantity and the liquer mix will be approximately 50% of the mother culture
	Day 4/5			
27	When specific gravity between 1.010 and 1.000 mother culture has carried out its function; proceed to bottling			take into consideration how much sugar you are going to add for the pressure required in your wine: 24g/l = 6bar at 10% ABV; 25g/l = 6bar at 11% ABV
28	Add sugar, riddling agents, nutrients, inactivated yeast as required			crown cap with bidule and shake before placing in a cage; ensure that the cage is sealed off from light in storage
29	Store the wine for a minimum of 9 months			do not store in a cold environment if recently started secondary fermentation – it will take approximately 6 weeks to complete

APPENDIX IV – RED WINE PRODUCTION TABLE

Serial	Winery Procedure	Addition	Typical Quantities	Remarks
	DAY 1			
1	Grapes arrive			log in the grape and weigh, note any imperfections in the fruit
2	Crush/destem into an open-top fermentation vessel	SO_2	40ppm	crush and destem as required – you may choose to whole-bunch press
3	Enzyme addition	add enzyme	1–2g/hl	maceration enzyme
4	Take sugar and acid readings and measure quantities			Oeschle and TA
5	Prepare bentonite		25g/hl	mix into a slurry in 10× its weight in water and settle for 24 hours
	DAY 2			
6	Cold maceration period			24–48 hours; if the fruit is not clean, add yeast straight away
7	Add bentonite	bentonite	25g/hl	
8	Take sugar and acid readings again	add sugar as required		17g/l will lead to 1% increase in ABV – aim for 12% ABV red wine
9	Add protecting nutrient	organic nutrient desirable	40g/hl	
10	Add yeast	Yeast	25g/hl	add a suitable yeast for your varietal
	NEXT 7 DAYS			
11	Punch down for the next 7 days, or until the fermentation ends			you may choose to pump over, just do not overdo it because of potential oxidation; fermentation temperature between 20° and 30°C
12	Monitor fermentation			use hydrometer and check for 'off' aromas – add DAP if any bad smells
13	Add nutrient	⅓ and ⅔ through fermentation	50g/hl	can be DAP or organic
14	Co-inoculate MLF bacteria if desired	MLF bacteria	cx instructions	ensure that your bacteria is designed for co-inoculation

15	Fermentation completion	SO_2 addition	40ppm	only add SO_2 if no MLF desired
16	MLF bacteria if desired	MLF bacteria	cx instructions	follow protocol if desired
17	Rack wine			
	Maturation			
18	Oak-barrel maturation	as desired		match weight of wine with oak – lighter style with older barrels
19	Stainles- steel maturation			
20	Check SO_2	SO_2 addition	40ppm	if not carrying out MLF add SO_2
21	Check protein stability			if not protein-stable, carry out fining trials
22	Cold stabilize	cooling jackets	100ml/hl	if you do not have cooling jackets fitted on your tanks, you will have to relay on time or cold weather, as CMC does not work on red wine
23	Final sugar additions			it may be necessary to add sugar to balance finished wine
24	Once protein- and cold-stable move to bottling stage			
25	Filter	earth or pad filter		
26	Final SO_2 checks		aim for 40ppm	no more than 40ppm free SO_2
27	Sterile filter and bottle			ensure sterility of all hoses and filling heads – if sterile bottling ensure 0.45µ

INDEX